Foreword by Neale Donald Walsch
(author of *Conversations with God*)

SANDY DONAGHY

THE

LONGEST
JOURNEY

*THE NINE KEYS TO HEALTH,
WEALTH AND HAPPINESS*

"A LIFE-CHANGING LITTLE, BIG BOOK"

This book is dedicated to my friend God, without whose help and inspiration this book would not have been possible.

It's also dedicated to my mother and father, my three brothers and my sister.

My spiritual mentors: Neale Donald Walsch and Em Claire who inspire me to greater heights by being just who they are: two lovely souls.

CONTENTS

AUTHOR'S NOTE

In September 1985, I was a homeless down-and-out living on the streets of Plymouth, Devon. I was given accommodation at a halfway house on the condition that I go to Alcoholics Anonymous to do something about my drinking. It was at this house I came across a book: *The Power of Positive Thinking* by Dr. Norman Vincent Peale. This book had what could best be described as an awakening for me. Almost instantly I wanted to change my life. I wanted to strive to be a better person.

I took up voluntary work at a local drop-in centre, which led me to do a counselling course. I enjoyed doing this course and soon noticed that it was helping me to help myself. So as you do, I decided to take a diploma course with the Central School of Counselling and Therapy in London. When I wrote my own life story I remembered that I had been on a spiritual journey for over 30 years.

Although my life was a disaster before coming into AA, there were things that I had achieved before alcohol won the battle. I was able to use all the things that I had learned over the years to good use in my journey along the spiritual path. I am so excited by my life today that words fail me. So together let us set out on the journey: the Longest Journey of all.

FOREWORD

Life is not easy for anyone. At least, no one I have met. It can become easy, but it is usually not easy to begin with. There are some things we have to learn. There are some tools we have to find. And there are some roads we have to travel.

Unless we can locate someone who has travelled them already, someone who knows the terrain, someone who can re-route us. Then we can gain from what they have learned.. Then we can use the tools they have found.

Ah, but connecting with such people—people who have done the hard lifting for us – is not easy. And so, most of us are left to take the journey alone.

Unless we are not.

Now by holding this book in your hand, you have ended that isolation. You are no longer alone, nor will have to be ever again. There is a man named Sandy Donaghy who has taken the journey already. He has taken the Longest Journey....and because he has, your own journey to peace, joy and fulfilment can be a great deal shorter. Sandy knowing all about how it is to have gotten there the hard way, the long way, can redirect you, helping you to get there the easy way, the shortest way.

Here he has broken down the path to just nine steps; Nine Keys to Health, Wealth and Happiness. Now you might think, Wait a minute. It can`t be that easy. But, in fact, it can be. If you use these keys one at a time, without skipping, without giving any of the steps short shrift, you can unlock the doors to the life for which you have yearned.

The great thing about this book is that on these pages Sandy talks right to you; it is like having him in the sitting here right in front of you, chatting amiably about some of the most important things you will ever explore. And so by, he makes the exploration easy.

But make no mistake about this....Sandy`s own life has been anything but easy. Indeed, his conversation with you begins with a description of what he thought was the end. I don`t want to say anything more about that, because I want you to have your own encounter with this terrific man and this terrific material. So I`ll leave it at saying that if you can put this book down after reading the first dozen paragraphs  or so of the opening section of this book—well you're a lot less interested in learning the secrets of turning one`s life around than I.

Neale Donald Walsch, Author of Conversations with God

INTRODUCTION

As a child I had a great imagination, and was influenced by the films that I saw. This influence was such that one day I would be John Wayne, the next Burt Lancaster. My idea of reality came from films, as did my teaching of romance. The only trouble with all this was that I learned how to do the courting part, but not how to live with someone full time. In the films they would just ride into the sunset. My relationships all did well at the courting stage, but failed at the living together part.

I was the third child of five and born on a Wednesday as well. Why, then, did I turn out to be such a mess? My brothers and sister didn't, yet we had the same upbringing. I don't really know the answer today, and furthermore it's not important – I just did. So I guess to summarise I was clueless about life and all its many facets.

Monday's child is full of grace.

Tuesday's child is fair of face.

Wednesday's child is full of woe.

Thursday's child has far to go.

Friday's child is loving and giving.

Saturday's child works hard for a living.

But the child that's born on the Sabbath day

Is bright, bonnie, good and gay!

Anonymous

So I was born on a Wednesday...

But not last Wednesday.

I have to hold my hands up to losing some great opportunities in my life. I have been blessed to meet some fabulous women; they have all tried hard to make their relationships work with me. If only I knew then what I know about myself now... who knows! In my working career I have managed to land some real good jobs with IBM, Plessey's and Racal's Electronics. If this is where you are right now, be of good cheer. You are now in a position to call a halt to all the chaos. NOW!

You have had the courage to admit all is not well in your life. That is the sort of courage that will get you through the Keys. One thing I can promise you is that you will spot the tools that you are using that just don't work anymore. Well, I ended up a homeless drunken tramp in the city of Plymouth in Devon, England. I think I will start from there to show you how the Nine Keys can transform your life, as they have mine.

THE BEGINNING

THE LONGEST JOURNEY

THE BEGINNING

Is it possible to have a good life? Can I change? How can a drunk like me be of any use to anyone! An ex-prison inmate, married twice, up to my eyes in debt – just what can I offer?

You're a failure, you're no good, you would be doing the world a favour if you killed yourself, but you can't even do that. Two failed suicide attempts already. This is God's punishment being administered to me. That vengeful God sitting on his high throne judging me...

These are just some of the thoughts I was having when I reached what Alcoholics Anonymous refer to as my rock bottom.

ROCK BOTTOM

I woke up one sunny September morning after sleeping behind the local Christian centre. I was hung over and really quite ill as a result of my alcoholism. I had met and was living with the 'ness' family: loneliness, fearfulness and hopelessness. I had reached what they talk of in Alcoholics Anonymous as my rock bottom.

I was riddled with fear and despair.

'I know what I will do,' I thought. 'I will end

this… Yes that's it… it's time to depart from
this terrible world… I don't belong here.'

It was a lovely morning in Plymouth. As I walked along the embankment, like a zombie, the water was still and there were not many people around. It was very early in the morning.

I picked up a rope and decided in my booze-crazed mind that I would hang myself… yes! That's the solution… I can't take any more.

I walked to an area known as Marsh Mills on the River Plym. I washed my face in the river, then sat down in the family picnic area. Soon families arrived. I sat and watched the children playing and enjoying their picnics. I wished that I had a normal life like that and yes, I was envious.

I suddenly realised that I was starving; I had not eaten in four days. My mind was repeating over and over again:

'This is all I ever wanted: a normal life.'

How had I ended up like this? I had not started out to be a homeless alcoholic.

Why? Why? Why? Where's God? I had searched for God since I was twenty and look at me now at forty-five.

I hate God. He is dead anyway… oh no! I had better not say that or I will be punished... I will end up in hell... but so what? I am in hell and according to the book of fear, the Bible, I was heading to hell anyway for what I was about to do.

Early evening when there was nobody about I decided it was time to exit this world. I walked into the woods to find a suitable tree to fix my rope to, making sure of course that it was not near a walkway as I did not want to be discovered by children. This was the thinking of my crazy mind.

I found a suitable tree and then to my horror discovered that the rope I was going to use was nylon and sort of elasticised. This rope was no use because it would leave a rope burn and furthermore I would end up going up and down like a yo-yo. I decided that I could not hang myself because I was a coward.

I walked back into Plymouth along the embankment, passing the church that I had slept behind the previous night. Two holy bouncers asked me to sign a petition to try and free a lady who had been arrested in a communist country for selling bibles. I signed the petition. They asked me if I wanted to go in for the service. I replied: 'No thanks, I have places to go.' They then said, 'We are having tea and sandwiches after.' 'Oh okay,' says I, and I went in.

The service is a bit of a blur, but I do remember answering the pastor's call for anyone who wanted saving to come forward. And I did. Why not? My life was a mess.

I was taken after the service to a halfway house.

Little did I know then that my life was about to change beyond my wildest dreams. I was about to begin a spiritual journey that would rocket me into the 4th dimension.

But first I had to free myself from the shackles of my past life. To do that I knew I needed Keys. I found those Keys and I am now passing on to you a tried and trusted method for changing your life. I will share some of my experiences with you in the hope they might be helpful. We will do them together.

'Each of us bears his own Hell'

Virgil (70-19 BCE)

That was then, this is now.

My life today is a richly rewarding experience. It is exiting. Each day is full of endless possibilities and challenges. But most of all I have a joy of living. What a turn around. I am so grateful for my life today. And it is all because I was prepared to go to any lengths to change my life, regardless of any pain I might have to undergo to achieve this.

My rock bottom was over twenty years ago, and since then I have undergone extensive therapy and counselling.

After reading endless self-help books offering amazing things, it was obvious to me that the majority of them were theoretically written by clean and polished individuals. Their life experiences were questionable. How, I wondered, could they write about subjects that they themselves had never experienced? And I observed that they were setting themselves up into little mutual appreciation societies, recommending each other's work. The media encourages this: picking out those with appropriate qualifications or high-sounding titles. It seemed to me that to be appreciated and considered worth listening to, you had to be a doctor or a professor. After all, they must know what they are talking about!

So this was my dilemma. Can I write a book? Have I anything constructive to offer? Can I offer hope to the millions who are struggling in today's world?

Then my soft inner voice whispered:

'You are, as we all are, a very special person and you have got a lot to offer. And yes, people will be interested in what you have to say.'

Why?

'BECAUSE IT IS YOUR TRUTH.
YOUR EXPERIENCES.'

I studied for four years to obtain a diploma in counselling. It was a great achievement for me. I am grateful to CSCT (Central School of Counselling and Therapy) and I am also grateful to a lady known as Fin who trained me in transactional analysis.

I have read countless books on religions: the Koran, the Bible, the Essenes, Sufi texts and the book of Mormon to name but a few.

I attended the local spiritualist church and discovered I had certain psychic abilities. I had an ability to administer spiritual healing. I was able to contact the other side. I am indebted to that church, as I am to all the churches I have attended, and I will talk about that later on.

There are many people who have influenced me, including Betty Shine, Watchman Nee, Dale Carnegie, M. Scott Peck, Diana Cooper, Gerald G. Jampolsky, Oprah Winfrey and Neale Donald Walsch. There are many more, too numerous to mention here.

MY FEAR OF GOD

The God I was familiar with was one of terror, retribution, murder and jealousy. God's job was to observe and condemn me. You're going to hell! Thou shall not! You sinful wretch! You are doomed! The various churches I have attended told me God is love... what!?

I have been baptised (out of my fear of God) about five times. I only had to walk down the road and hear some preacher or layman say, 'Ours is the only true faith' and within hours I would be in the water... saved again! What a life!

I was terrified of God, which was a by-product of the Scottish school system. My earliest memory of the God of terror was when I was around nine years of age. The school were all route marched to the local Church of Scotland for the Christmas service. It was bitterly cold and snow had just fallen. To be in short pants was not recommended.

The church was freezing and dimly lit, and the minister was so high up in his rostrum I thought he was God. And he preached of doom and gloom, pointing his bony finger at us... thou shall NOT! The highlight of the service for me was nicking a ten-bob note out of the collection plate as it was passed around. It was sweetie time... yes! And a happy Christmas was had by all.

The God of my understanding at that time filled my heart with fear and guilt. I was emotionally crippled as a result of my experiences of God.

I discovered through therapy that my belief system had played a big part in my life being one of frustration and misery. How do you tell God to clear off and leave you alone?

I had let go wonderful relationships through fear and guilt of displeasing God. I can't live with this female: it's a sin! I can't do this or that: it's a sin! Sin! Sin! I am sick of it. How do I get rid of God? How can I get God out of my life... leave me alone! I read somewhere that you get rid of an idea by creating a new idea. This seemed like sense to me. I realised it was going to take a lot of courage.

Courage is the magic word... oh yeah! I was frightened of my shadow. How do you get courage? Courage was something I lacked in most areas of my life. But you can't go to the local supermarket and say: 'A bag of courage please.' They would re-direct you to the alcohol section... would they not? That's all I needed. No! Somehow I had to change my belief system and my attitude to life. But how?

I worked at a local drop-in centre for four years. My clients suffered from domestic violence, anger problems, violence, fear and lack of self worth.

This was a terrific learning situation for me. I learned so much about myself. I also began to formulate a system to help the clients to help themselves.

It has taken me twenty years to finally come up with a system that anyone can use to change his or her life. One that works. It worked for me, it will for you.

THE ONLY REQUIREMENTS ARE:

1. Wanting to change your life.

2. Being prepared to be honest with yourself.

3. Following the system as it is laid out.

You are in shackles from your past. Here are some of the shackles that were binding me and destroying my life.

MY BELIEF SYSTEM

I was not worthy of God.

I was a sinner.

I was a coward.

I was unlike-able.

I was useless.

I was a drain on society.

I would never amount to much.

I must not trust people.

I must look after number one.

I must take what I want, no matter the cost.

I must never trust woman: they are all liars.

This is the belief system I was using. This is the system that created my life, right to my rock bottom.

HOW ABOUT YOU?

What misconceived life system led you to this book? Why is your life not all that you had hoped for? What went wrong? What happened to your dreams?

It may seem a very strange thing to hear, but you do have all the answers. They are buried under life or your experience of life up to this point.

I think it would be safe to say things are not good for you at this moment in time. Well, you need to find the problem... I mean the deep-rooted problem. The chances are if you were to receive a cheque today you would still deep down be unhappy. Yes, you could pay the bills, have a holiday and for a while all would be well in your world.

But it will not be long before your life starts to take a dive for the worse. Why? Because you are operating on a false system and you are wrongly programmed. The false beliefs are the shackles that are binding you. They will always win. They are deeply rooted in you, as they once were in me.

Did you notice I said: ONCE WERE?

They are no more. You can change your life too. I am just an average guy; I am what we term in this country 'working class'. So if I can transform my life, there is no reason for you not to do the same.

I have developed a system that has worked on many of my clients. A system that works, and one that does not require you to have a degree to understand how it works.

We are shackled to our past. To unlock those shackles and free yourself, you need a set of Keys. I have developed those Keys... they work and here they are:

NINE KEYS TO A NEW LIFE

Key One: Write a Life Story
Key Two: Find a Higher Power
Key Three: Forgiveness
Key Four: Change
Key Five: Gratitude
Key Six: Attraction
Key Seven: Design Your Life
Key Eight: The Journey Begins
Key Nine: 24 Hours is Lifetime

Does it all look daunting to you? Not to worry. As I stated earlier I will go through the Keys with you. I will share some of my experiences dealing with the Keys.

Take a breather. You are about to undergo a life-changing pro-gramme. Your life may be a mess, but all that is about to change. You have already taken a major step forward in your life. You are reading this book. You are looking for something to help you change your life; look no further – you have found it.

Are you ready to do some work? Are you willing to give this your best shot?

OK. Fasten your seat belt: here we go.

THE JOURNEY BEGINS

What journey? You may be wondering.

A journey into the self.

You are about to transform your life.

Happiness is on its way.

You are one special person.

> *'There is no cure for birth and death,*
> *save to enjoy the interval.'*
>
> *(George Santayana 1863- 1952)*

KEY ONE

WRITE YOUR LIFE STORY

KEY ONE

WRITE YOUR LIFE STORY

Why would I want to do that? I hear you mumble. For me this was very, very, important. It was a starting point. Hey! I knew my life was a mess, I was experiencing the bad feelings and I was depressed. But I asked the question: what brought me to this point in time? Had anything happened in my past to create this situation today? I was experiencing the symptoms, but had no idea of the root cause.

This exercise was so very beneficial to me that I cannot emphasise its importance strongly enough. Yeah! How?

Well I discovered many issues in my past that were directly affecting me today – some forty years on. Did you hear that? Some forty years on.

There were many skeletons in my cupboard. There were many forms of abuse: verbal and sexual. I also discovered my past programming. The information I was given by parents and other adults. What I was told to remember programmed information that was intended to help and protect me from the outside world. Here are a few examples of what I mean:

'Don't go to the ballet! They are a load of queers.' 'Don't tell anyone outside what goes on in this house.' 'Stay away from Catholics, they are evil.'

And of course they're many prophetic quotes. Here are some of them:

'You will never amount to anything.' 'You will end up like your father (he was rather to fond of alcohol).' 'You are thick.' 'You will end up a lonely man.' Oops!

Do you get the picture? Do you now understand the importance of writing your life story? It is a minefield of information.

And in my case it showed me quite clearly the root causes of the life I had created for myself. It will also do this for you – provided you have the ability to be honest.

WARNING

Do not adopt the 'it won't work for me' attitude. Be positive with yourself. Don't have 'contempt prior to investigation.'

Reserve all judgemental opinions until you have at least tried the Keys in your life.

Stop reading. Put the book down.

We cannot carry on until you have written your own life story.

TIPS ON WRITING YOUR LIFE STORY

For some of you this task may be easy, but for others rather daunting. I had to write 42 years down. Half the time in the finish I could not remember where I had been, let alone what I had done. I struggled with this task until a moment of clarity arrived. I remembered I always liked music and was the one who always put music on the jukebox if there were one. I noticed if I heard a tune I could associate with it, and I remembered what I was doing and where I was when that specific record was out.

I then went to the local library and got hits from the fifties up to the eighties. Listening to the music was like having direct access to my life records. I could see myself at the time of the music, where I was and what was happening in my life at that time. There was a record recorded by Bob Hope called 'A Four-legged Friend' that took me back to when I was five, sitting in front of a fire licking a lollipop and reading the Beano comic. That is how powerful music has been and still is in my life.

So I started writing my story from aged five. It is quite amazing what information your brain stores. I was able to get in touch with Sandy as a child; I could recall events in my life clearly. The whole experience for me was simply wonderful and in the end so liberating.

A timely reminder: the whole exercise is not to apportion blame, but to discover why you react the way you do as an adult.

I was quite surprised how I made it this far using the tools that I thought were so effective, but in reality were so destructive. The good news for me and for you is that once you clearly identify the tools that are causing you heartache, you can change them and can install new ones. You can begin probably for the first time to truly take control of your life.

It is true to say that for many this story writing can bring up some horrible memories. Perhaps incidents that you have buried for years are suddenly seeing the light of day. The feelings this will bring up will be very painful. If I can make a suggestion here, whilst you are writing your story it is helpful to have some form of support behind you: perhaps a priest, minister, pastor or a dear friend you can trust to share the emotions coming up. I like the saying:

You are only as sick as your secrets.

Once a secret meets the light of day it loses its power over you. It is the beginning of victory over your life.

Others may prefer to write their story in columns. It does not matter what method you use as long as it is a method that is comfortable for you. It's not a test, there are no grades awarded. It is simply digging at the roots to clear away the pus and allow healing to take place. Do not minimise the courage you are showing at this point in your life. This is true courage, believe me.

Another tip that you may find useful is to reward yourself by being nice to you. You have had enough pain and sadness to last you another lifetime, so be gentle with you – you are a very special person indeed and a child of the universe.

Further into this book we will discover who we really are. We are not the person that we think we are at this present moment, the failure, the no hoper, the waste of space, a walking disaster etc.

Well! What did you discover about yourself? Did anything come screaming out at you? I wish now to applaud your courage in writing your story. Yes! I said courage.

After I had written my story I suddenly understood what true courage was about. It was not, as I had thought, about how tough you were with other people or how macho you behaved.

Writing your own life story is the first Key. The question is: what do you do with it now that you have written it? You will need to analyse it. Have a look to see repetitive behaviour that has resulted in bad outcomes for you. What are the triggers that produce these behaviours?

Try to find how old you were when you started to use these behaviours. Why did you start to use such destructive patterns of behaviour?

When I was very young and I did something wrong and was asked by my parent: 'Was this you?' I said, 'Yes' and I got a clip round the ear. From that moment I adopted the defence:

Honesty equals punishment.

I carried that through my life and it caused me nothing but heartache. Money was very scarce in my house and it was held as the number one commodity. So my fear of financial insecurity was fostered during those days.

Here is another example of how my fear of lack of money affected my life as a child. It was Christmas Eve and my mother asked me to go down to the shops and get a Christmas tree. It was snowing outside and had been falling all day. She wrapped the money in a piece of newspaper. I fetched my imaginary horse (I was only nine) and set off in the snow to the shops. On the way I encountered some outlaws and a tribe of Indians, so after three battles I finally reached the shops and... no money! I had lost the money. A fate worse than death awaited me. I remember walking home in tears. What am I going to tell my mum, oh boy I am in for it.

I hit on an idea to get me out of this situation without telling my mother – after all, honesty equals punishment. I called on one of our neighbours and said, 'My mother sent me down to borrow some money as we don't have any for Christmas.' This poor woman who had six children gave me ten bob (50p). And off I went again to the shops and got a Christmas tree and spent the change on sweets.

We had a good Christmas. It was sometime in February when I had just parked my horse. I came in the house and got a real hammering from my mother. The lady I had borrowed ten bob (50p) from had approached her in a shop and asked if she could pay it back! This all happened because of my fear of punishment and my fear of financial insecurity.

My thinking was wrong and was driving my life in adulthood. I could plainly see this in my life story. So you see, writing your life story can and does highlight incorrect thinking and beliefs.

So you need to look for recurring cycles of behaviour that no longer serve you. It is frightening how these childhood impressions so distort your life. I always fell short in relationships, especially if there was any hint of not enough money. I would be like a bat out of hell.

So make lists of what frightened you as a child. What made you unhappy? Who hurt you and why? And on the other side, what were the great times like? Who was always kind to you?

Try to glean as much information as you can from your story. Take your time. This is probably the hardest thing you have attempted to do in your life, and you only have to do this once.

I think we are in agreement that if you don't know what's

wrong in your life you can't fix it. Make no mistake: you are going to transform your life. So do the best you can with your life story – it is a minefield of information. Yes! It can be painful sifting through your life, but you need only do this once.

Like I said, I discovered so much about myself. It is a miracle that I reached the age I am, relatively in one piece.

I discovered that my life was driven by fear. I was fearful of God, fearful of financial insecurity, I was fearful of commitment, I was fearful of the truth, I was fearful of dying, I was fearful of living. I found out that all the disastrous situations I found myself in were due to fear.

Can you imagine trying to live a happy life with these anchors on you? It is no longer a surprise or a mystery to me that my life was a disaster and also for those who got involved with me.

I felt really sorry for the people that I had harmed in my life. But most of all I was sorry for this child who had never grown up.

But now I know the reasons why my life was a mess. It was from the point of knowing that I could begin the healing process. And it is from this same point that you can start to heal. So I can't emphasise the importance of the life story enough.

The only reason that I share with you some of my life experiences is that you may also be able to turn your life around, as I have. I am so concerned for my fellow humans that I will do what ever I can to help them to help themselves.

It is you that is doing the work and by the same token it is you who will get the benefits of an honest appraisal of your life.

If you are finding this all a bit daunting then perhaps this suggestion may be of benefit to you. Break the story down into decades, 1-10 years, 10-20 years etc. and analyse each decade. Be brave, admit your wrongdoings and don't hide anything. If you are to get the desired result, you will need to be courageously honest with yourself. This is an exercise between you and you and is private to you. There is no need not to be honest.

Well! What did you discover about yourself? Did anything come screaming out at you? I wish now to applaud your courage in writing your story. Yes! I said courage.

After I had written my story I suddenly understood what true courage was about. It was not, as I thought, about how tough you were with other people. How macho you behaved. I had created a wall around myself. You know what I mean: don't come too close... no one is going to hurt me.

Now! What can I do with this information?

This feels like a big job. It feels a bit frightening. I need help.

The question is what kind of help? Who can help me? Who can I trust? And that gentle voice in my head started saying:

Know that I am God and be still.

KEY TWO

FIND A POWER GREATER THAN YOU

KEY TWO

FIND A POWER GREATER THAN YOU

Oh no, not him again… anything but that! Will you leave me alone!

Know that I am God and be still.

I had discovered in my life story that I was having a love-hate relationship with this God. Deep inside of me I knew there had to be something more to life than what I was experiencing.

In my life I discovered that I had many times tried to get close to God. As my story revealed to me, these attempts always ended in more fear and pain and in disaster. I just did not fit in with any of the congregations and their do-goody mentality. The experience always felt controlling, but with a smile. Members all seeking positions of power, or as I would say today: control. You are welcome here, but you must not do any of the following… ugh!… get off my case. So to try and find a higher power was for me no mean task.

I remember saying to myself: 'Well, you do have the courage to stand up for yourself. Challenge this God.' What does it matter if the threat of hell is issued? I have been in hell for a long time. Of course this brave outburst was tinged with fear. This all happened twenty years ago, don't forget.

And so I embarked on my spiritual journey to find out more about God.

I began by reading spiritual books of all descriptions and persuasions. But my strangest experiences were to be had when I started visiting churches.

I got the distinct impression that I was not all together welcome, and after a while the congregation was glad to get rid of me. I was outspoken and my internal dialogue was coming up with some weird stuff.

I would say things like: 'I reckon we have it wrong. If we were with God before we came into physical being that surely means we died to come here.' We left paradise to come here! Sounds like death to me.

And we are told that after death we return (if we are good little boys and girls of course, and have pleased God) to heaven… that sounds like birth to me and we move into paradise. At one of the church home meetings there was a lot of wailing and gnashing of teeth concerning, 'Is God happy with us? Are we doing the right work?' Enter my now familiar internal voice:

No! You are doing more harm than good. You are turning people away with your arrogance and

self-centeredness. You are adhering to the mes-
senger and forgetting the message: LOVE.

So out I came with that message. You could have heard a pin drop. Then the pastor coughed gently and spoke a very profound statement: 'Who do you think you are?' Enter the voice:

'God so loved the world that he sent me.'

End of the home group for me. Don't misunderstand me here; I have absolutely nothing against religions or spiritual people. I just did not fit into the established churches (I have tried most of them, as I said earlier). But the most wonderful thing for me personally was that I was becoming aware of a power greater than me, within me… wow! So what do I believe today? I believe that God talks to everyone all the time without exception.

And I understand the Lord's statement:

'He who has ears to hear, let him hear.'

Mark 4, Verse 9

I am at peace today with the God of my understanding; She is my best friend and I love Him. The war is over, and that feels good to me. There is no one better than me and no one worse than me and that is another great feeling. We are all one with the universe. I will do anything I can to help my brother or sister: I believe if I help them I help myself.

So we need to believe in something or someone greater than us. We need to find a higher power and the God of our understanding. Why? Because we need to heal ourselves. We need to learn to forgive and receive forgiveness.

I don't know about you, but when I was in charge of my life I ended up a drunken homeless tramp. So are you prepared to hand your will and your life over to a God of your understanding? At least try it. You need the rest; you have been in the driving seat too long. Come in out of the cold. Meet with the God of love, the God of compassion and the God of forgiveness.

This God is not on some throne somewhere judging you from afar. The God of love is within you. Yes! That's right! Within you. Is it not written?

'The kingdom of heaven is within you.'

I don't know about you, but I can tell you about me. I was a beaten man. My thinking and my planning for my life had produced disastrous results. There must be something wrong with my thinking and there was. I thought I was alone in the world. I felt alien to this world. I just did not fit. My feelings were dead, I was numb to anything. I had no get up and go about me. I lacked energy. Everything was an effort. I was deeply lonely, I could feel myself crying inside, yet still smiling to the outside world.

I would go out during the day and meet people. They would ask me, 'How do you feel?' 'Great! Just great thanks. How are you?' I would look at what appeared to be happy people and wonder if they were really crying inside like me.

I knew I was going to have to put my trust in the God of my understanding. I had come to the end of the road. I was in my own garden of Gethsemane. I said:

'Father I turn my will and my life over to you. Do what you will with me. Thy will, not mine, be done.'

This Key is so vital to grasp and take action on that I cannot stress its importance enough. Look at your life story. Can you see what happened when you were in charge? So what or who is this higher power that we need to come to terms with?

This is a very personal issue and a very important one. Your future depends on you finding some power greater than you to relate to. I know a lot of people who have had great difficulty with this Key, but have eventually come to believe in the God of their own understanding.

So if you have no understanding of a power greater than you, how can you change that opinion? A lot of people get mixed up with spirituality and religion. I like the quote I heard:

Religion is for those who are afraid of going to hell and spirituality is for those who have been to hell.

A good starting point in the quest to find a higher power can be taking a walk in the countryside. Look at the abundance of nature. Look at all the trees, bushes, flowers, streams and look at the people who pass you by. What do you see?

There are none so blind as those who will not see.

The variety of nature can be quite overwhelming. Look up to the heavens on a clear night and witness the celestial show, visible to all. Consider the vastness of it all: the universe is an astonishing canvas full of design and character. Where do you fit in the order of things?

Are we just insignificant beings blown around in the winds of circumstance or, as others might say, fate? I do not believe that these days. But this is not about me, it is about you. So is there a lesson for us all in nature?

'A soul who is not close to nature is far away from what is called spirituality. In order to be spiritual one must communicate, and especially one must communicate with nature; one must feel nature.'

The Sufi message of Hazrat Inayat Khan, in

The Art of Personality

In that quotation I think it is abundantly clear that nature is the perfect starting point in your quest to find a higher power.

The seasons are another feature of life that is worth looking at with a keener eye and an open heart. Winter, spring, summer and autumn. No matter what we do or think, the seasons are dependable and function perfectly without our input. The seasons come and go regardless of how we are feeling! Why?

There are laws in the universe that organise the constellations. All life seems to be governed by a hidden force. There is something we don't quite understand about the life around us. We have been to the moon and are reaching further into space, probing other planets and constellations. What, I wonder, do we hope to find? Are we searching for other signs of intelligent life, or some other planet to inhabit?

Mankind seems always to be searching for new frontiers, new horizons. All through history man has challenged the confines of his world and gone searching for new lands, new cultures, new riches and new conquests. Why do we do those things? I believe it is our inherent nature; something deep inside of us informs us that there is more to life than what we may perceive. What lies beyond that stretch of water? What lies behind that mountain? It seems we can never be content with our lot. We have to spend time wondering whether the grass really is greener in the other field.

It seems to me that in actual fact we are constantly seeking change. Nature shows us that change is the very essence of life;

the prerequisite for life. Nothing in nature stands still: have you noticed that? Everything is in a state of constant change. We, on the other hand, cling dearly to what we have and fear change in our lives. I want things to remain as they are; at least I know where I am with how things are with me.

Is this the same for you, I wonder? Change is the very thing that is going to release you from a life of misery and move you to one of happiness. So how are you now regarding a higher power? I think we have proven the point that nature is a power greater than you. So you now have a starting point. Remember, we all breathe the same air; we are all dependent on air to stay alive. So we are also a part of nature, just as assuredly as the animals are. There is a cosmic link with all life – without air what are we? So in my life I go through the seasons: birth, teenager, adult, old age, that is how I choose to look at my life. In a good way it is very reassuring for me to accept this principle. All aspects of living, including death, are simply the rhythm of life. The law of life if you will. Therefore there is nothing to fear but fear itself. So I think with what we have talked about here, there is no problem finding a power greater than ourselves... is there?

There is great comfort to be had when you accept your own mortality. When you can see and understand that you are not the centre of the universe, simply a part of the universe. Life does not revolve around you, and we are in fact all dependant on each other. The pressure is taken from you when you can accept that the universe conspires to help you all the time.

Well, if nature has not helped you to find the God of your own understanding, let's try quantum physics. What? I hear you say! Quantum physics! Science has come a long way since I was at school. It is now a matter of fact that science has come up with this theory.

The universe arose in what is often referred to as the 'Big Bang'. So the universe arose and gave rise to the galaxies. The galaxies gave rise to the stars. Our sun gave rise to life and all that we are.

'To tell the story of anything, you have to tell the story of everything.'

Thomas Berry PhD, cultural historian

'We are all one, we are all connected and we all came from the same source. There is a profound wisdom at work in the universe.'

Drew Dellinger, poet and teacher

Therefore, we are all cosmological beings. We are all interrelated. There is a profound kinship with everything. We are all related by energy and genetics. We are one with each other, whether that other is an ape or a butterfly. According to science this planet of ours was once molten rock. The rock cooled and the earth began to clothe itself in life. What an astounding fact that is. Think about it. From molten rock to the lush planet we call earth and home. That is what I call a miracle. What do you think? I am not a scientist and I am drawing my information from documentaries and books. But this is another avenue for understanding that there is a power greater than you at work.

I hope looking at nature and the universe has been of help to you in finding the God of your understanding. This is the only reason I have mentioned these topics. It is so important to find a higher power that you are comfortable with. The rest of the programme depends on this.

When I finally accepted the higher power of my own understanding, life became so much easier for me, and it will for you. I came to believe that anything was possible in my life. I suddenly tapped into the greatest unused force in the universe and things began to change for the better in my life. It will for you as you work the other Keys into your life.

> *'May God steal from you all*
> *that steals you from him.'*
>
> Rabia'a Al-Adawiyya (717-809)

'The spirit came from God and will return to God.
The present life is only a moment in between.'

Jalal Al-Din Rumi (1207-1273)

'God is in thy heart, yet thou searchest
for him in the wilderness.'

Arjun (1563-1606)

'God is within you, but we place
Him outside and worship him.'

Yogaswami (1872-1964)

Well I think we have explored sufficient avenues in order to find a power greater than ourselves. All that is required of us now is to accept there is a power greater than us. That we need to give this higher power a chance in our lives. Let's put Her to the test, let's give ourselves a break from being at the helm of the bridge and allow our lives to be guided by this higher power. After all, what do we have to lose?

Your life at present is not the way you wish it to be – otherwise why are you reading this book? We now clearly see the disaster our lives had become when we were in charge. It is time now to make the commitment to hand your life over to the care of a power greater than you: your higher power.

Congratulations! You are now under a different influence, and you have a different driving force in your life. You are now awake. There is nothing you cannot achieve with the guidance of the God of your understanding.

> *'I said you are God's, and all of you*
> *are children of the most high.'*

Psalm 82, Verse 6

From this moment forward you are on the journey you were always meant to be on: the journey into the self. All possibilities now exist in your life to recreate anew that which you want to be.

It would truly be naïve of you to expect that everyone in your life is going to accept your newly found approach to life. They have probably heard this 'never again' cry from you before. There will probably be consequences of your past life to address and issues to be resolved. You might ask yourself: 'how do you eat an elephant?' The answer:

> *One bite at a time.*

YOUR ELEPHANT

Now there are many ways to reduce your elephant to edible bites. They normally fall into three brackets: financial, emotional and spiritual.

FINANCIAL

The first principle is to cease being the ostrich and to remove your head out from under the sand.

I was told to make a list of all my debts, putting everything down. The next step was to calculate my income. Then deduct from my income the amount I needed for electricity, gas, hygiene, rent or mortgage, telephone, food and travel costs etc. When I had calculated my total living costs and subtracted them from my income I was left with the money I could start to clear my debts with.

This process will be different for most of us, depending on our current status. Let's say for example I owed money to ten people. I would divide the money I had to pay my debts by ten. The figure I was left with was what I would be able to offer my debtors. I was told then to write a letter to all ten people offering to pay my debt at x amount each week or month.

The most amazing thing happened to me. My debtors accepted my offer. I was now financially stable for the first time in years.

EMOTIONAL

I think it would be true to say that we have all experienced emotional pain in our lives. To be told that most of my emotional pain was down to my *perception* of the event was hard to swallow. But it was an eye opener at the same time. When I read my life story I could see certain things that pointed to this idea being true for me. I was a drama queen, staggering from one emotional disaster to the next hoping things would be different next time. How could they be? I had not changed. I was still being driven by the same childhood scripts – the ones that were causing me pain after pain, and are doing the same for you.

For me. the emotional holocaust eased when I started to change my life and change the demands I made on my life.

But there was one thing staring me in the face and I saw it coming. I had to start to learn how to forgive, and how to come off my high horse and to learn to say 'sorry', and what's more mean it.

SPIRITUALLY

We addressed the issue of finding a higher power. And this brings us to the end of Key Two.

Why not go and do something nice just for you. You certainly deserve to.

KEY THREE

FORGIVENESS

KEY THREE

FORGIVENESS

*'Forgiveness is letting go of all
hopes for a better past.'*

'Forgiveness releases us from the painful past.'

*'You either totally forgive or
you do not forgive at all.'*

*(All the above quotations are by Gerald G. Jampolsky, MD, from
the book* Forgiveness: the Greatest Healer of All.*)*

Forgiveness is an avenue for checking out your true courage status. Am I brave enough to forgive?

I had a difficult time with forgiveness. There were some people I would never forgive. Hell would freeze over before that happened. I soon learned that I could not properly forgive anybody until I first learned to forgive myself.

Then I read somewhere that medically speaking it would be very healthy and therapeutic to my system if I adopted the tool of forgiveness. And so I forgave myself for hurting me. I wept for hours after I did this. It was so cleansing and I felt so much lighter in myself for doing this. It is a must to do this before tackling those other areas where forgiveness will be required.

Forgiving is really a two-sided Key – the other side is being willing to apologise and apologising to those you can. Those you have harmed physically, mentally or any other way. From your life story you can make such a list. Get used to using those holy words:

I am sorry, please forgive me.

What you are doing and what I have done is to begin to clear away the debris of the past. If you like we are starting life over with a new tool bag, containing a new set of tools.

REMEMBER:

You are no longer in charge of your life: the God of your understanding is. Once you can really believe this and feel this deep within, you will see your life transformed. The struggle is over. There is a truce with the world. You will be amazed at how doors begin to open up for you. New ideas and directions for your life will appear, as if by magic.

Your load has been lightened; you will begin to feel free. You will know what your life has been like up to this moment. You will have discovered things about yourself that have been buried under anger, tears, fear, heartache, pain and sorrow. You will clearly see what you like and what you dislike about yourself. You will want to change the dislikes. You will begin to experience a peace that is deep rooted. You will probably wonder: how can this be, considering the life I have lived? As you continue working the Keys, your understanding of many things will expand. You will see yourself in wonder.

Forgiveness is a very important concept: it is the beginning of healing. What a wonderful gift from the universe healing is. By now you will probably see clearly that you can do nothing about your circumstances until you do something about you. It all starts with you.

Remember you are the cause of your current situation. Therefore, conversely, you are the creator of your new life. It is you that has the blank blackboard, and you can write whatever you want for yourself and how you want your life to be.

But before you can honestly achieve this you, like me, need to heal. What do we need to heal? How do we set about healing? What does healing really mean? And why is it paramount to our new desired way of living?

Well, simply put you cannot sew a new patch on old clothes. This means you have to address your old ideas. The ideas that have got your life to the present state. The idea here is not to punish yourself; you have done enough of that. It is simply to acknowledge that your best thinking has resulted in the situation you find yourself in today.

So make a list of wrong decisions and their consequences. Own this list and thank the universe for all that has occurred thus far in your life. And now proclaim how you want your life to be and the new principles you wish to use in your life from this moment onwards.

Look at yourself with compassion and love. Forgive yourself for the hurt you may have caused. Acknowledge how life was before you came to accept a power greater than you into your life. And rejoice in the fact that you are no longer alone. You have a power that will never reject you, condemn, punish or abandon you.

How does that feel?. For me it was an overwhelming feeling. I knew that my life was going to change for the better. I did not know how. Deep inside of me there was a feeling of relief and peace, even amongst all the chaos I had caused.

If it happened for me it will happen for you, and this is why I decided to write this book. I know how my life has been transformed from one of fear and anger to one of love and compassion. If I can help one soul turn their life around my dream will have been fulfilled.

This is not an ego trip for me. This is my compassion and desire to do my bit to help my fellow human. To help promote hope in a world of chaos. To help shine a light in the darkness. To inform my fellow souls that we are loved beyond our imagination. We are magnificent just as we are.

So I started to be nice to me (something I had not done for a long time), and this is what you must now practise. I used to give myself a treat everyday, something just for me. I had very little money but I could treat myself to a bubble bath, and just soak in it, feeling the warmth engulf my body. It was great. Then I progressed to a bubble bath with candles and spiritual music in the background and that was fabulous. I progressed to treating myself to a cake and a cappuccino. I used to go to the library and take out a self-help book, and practise reading some uplifting words each day. I began to open my mind to other philosophies. Read about beliefs and religions. Try to walk in other people's steps for a while. I began, slowly at first, to become excited about life.

It was like breaking the surface of a river having been under the water for forty years, and seeing the beauty of my surroundings. Everything looked different; cleaner if you will. It is hard to see the beauty of the forest when you are entrenched and lost in it. I could see only my problems. I could think of nothing else. I would wallow in self-pity. I was dying, not physically but spiritually. My emotions were all but dead, and they were certainly damaged.

I started the book informing you of my rock bottom, but rock bottoms take many forms. You could be a millionaire and be in your rock bottom, rich in money and material things but void of spirituality and love. That feels equally terrible to me. You could be on the outside happily married but empty inside – equally terrible. You could be in a job you really hate, but out of necessity you have to do it. That sounds terrible to me. You can't see any light at the end of the tunnel, which is a horrible, terrible place to be. You could be old and beginning to wonder what life was all about – what have you done with it? What was the point? Did I do the right thing and so forth. This is a very lonely place to be.

So rock bottoms are simply what an individual determines is enough for them. It is a wake up call if you will. But where is this call coming from? It is coming from your deepest self, and it is coming from the real you. The God-like part of you. It is from your soul. Your soul has brought you to this point. Why? To remind you who you really are. To awaken you to the limitless possibilities there are in your life. It is simply saying... stop! This is not how your life was meant to be. You are not here to suffer, that was never the plan. It is the result of greed, bullying, fear and manipulation that the world is where it is today.

There is not enough to go round!

You must beat the other guy!

Look after number one!

Hoard all you can for a rainy day!

Kill those who threaten your way of living!

Punish those who do not live as you want them to!

Don't trust! Sod the rules! Etc., etc. etc.

Is all this familiar to you? You would have to be living on another planet not to see the result of this thinking. So you see the whole world needs healing and it starts with you and I healing us. You can't give away what you don't have, can you?

So I personally think that healing and forgiveness are one of the same and go hand in hand. Try it – truly forgive someone and then monitor how you feel about this. You will feel lighter and happier and healed with that soul. It's as simple as that. So let's have a recap on our situation now. We have written our life story, come to believe in a power greater than us and are now learning about forgiveness – why we need to forgive and how to go about it. We can clearly see the urgent need to start to treat ourselves, and to look after our physical and spiritual selves. To let go... oops! Where did that come from? Well let's have a look at letting go.

LETTING GO

Letting go simply put means to leave the past, once you have addressed it fairly and squarely, in the past. Do not spend valuable time dwelling there. There is no need to re-enact events over and over again. How does it profit you to do this? I know this is not an easy thing to do. It takes practise, and yes, discipline to change your thinking, but if I can do it I believe you can as well. When I am playing music and I don't like a track I simply skip that track to a track that I do like. On my computer if I see something I do not like, I simply delete it. I had to learn or rather practise doing that with my thoughts. If I found myself thinking thoughts of the past, I would thank my mind for them but say, 'this is not what I want to think about', and replace my thoughts with positive ones. It sounds a bit barmy I know, but it worked for me and for the people I have been blessed to help. So try it, and then decide what is good for you.

Let's take a break. Let's do something we have not done for a long time: let's say thank you to the God of our understanding. Thank you for my life. Thank you for my family. Thank you for my friends. Thank you for my trials. Thank you for this day. Thank you for my uniqueness. Thank you for the flowers. Thank you for the birds. Thank you for the animals. Thank you for this world. Thank you for everyone in it. Thank you for the breathtaking universe.

Feels good doesn't it? And hey, guess what? While you were offering your thanks you were not thinking of you. You were giving your overworked brain a rest, and boy does it need a rest. There is a universal secret contained here.

When you think of others, you give yourself a rest.

Are you beginning to see light at the end of the tunnel? Are you beginning to have some hope? Can you see a better life? Can you visualise a new life for yourself? You should by now understand that you are taking control, nay, responsibility for your life. The mess will disappear when you work through these Keys. The truth is you have probably got nothing to lose by trying the Keys. The reason is not important – the action is the only requirement for you to change your life as this shows a desire for you to want to. And if you are still reading this book you have the desire. Do you have the honesty? Without that you are blowing in the wind. You are only shortcoming yourself if you lie. This leads us neatly to Key Four: Change.

KEY FOUR

☼

CHANGE

KEY FOUR

CHANGE

Lord,

Make me an instrument of your peace,

Where there is hatred let me sow love;

Where there is injury, pardon;

Where there is doubt, faith;

Where there is despair, hope;

Where there is darkness, light, and

Where there is sadness, joy.

O divine master;

Grant that I may not so much

Seek to be consoled as to console;

To be understood as to understand;

To be loved as to love.

For it is in giving that we receive;

It is in forgiving that we are forgiven;

It is in dying that we are born to eternal life.

(Prayer attributed to St. Francis of Assisi)

In that prayer is the recipe for change, and the high ideals we are aiming for. When I first read the prayer I was moved to tears.

Having made a list of the things I did not like about myself e.g. arrogance, pride, intolerance, lust, fear, greed, spite, manipulative tendencies, meanness, bad manners, envy and a host of other defects (I think you should have the idea by now) I set about asking the God of my understanding to help me remove these defects, and to give me the strength and courage to change my life. I received this strength and so will you.

God, grant me the serenity

To accept the things I cannot change,

(people, places and things)

Courage to change the things I can,

(myself)

And the wisdom to know the difference.

So let's recap on the journey so far. By now you should have used the first four Keys. An idea of how your life can and will change should be forming. You should be feeling like you have had a shower on the inside.

The world may already be looking less hostile to you. You could also feel quite strange and slightly empty. You may even feel quite flat.

Don't worry, this is all perfectly normal. I would ask you just to walk in faith, believing that things are going to change for the better soon… believe me, they are.

THE WORLD

One's perception of the world is very important. It can seem to be a very hostile planet, and reading newspapers can confirm that. It is a fact that bad news is more interesting than good news in the media's eyes. When I was struggling with change, this understanding of the world kept me in fear.

It also used to give me the mind-set of 'What's the point in trying to change? We could be at war tomorrow.' No matter what I tried to do there was this mind-set hanging over me. The turning point for me was when I reduced the world to my world. Instead of worrying about the various hostilities and the constant violent crime in the world, and instead of allowing what could be to run my life, I reduced it to what *is* my world.

MY WORLD

It was a very revealing exercise. This is one that I would recommend you to do. I actually reduced my world to the size that it really was. I lived on an estate of about 700 houses. I only knew four people on the estate. I did not have any idea about the other 696 families. I socialised with about eight people. My life revolved around these people. I lived in a suburb of a city, only going into the city three or four times a week. I never attended the theatre or cinema, or went out for a meal. My world reduced the real world to about 15 square miles. Very small in the scope of things, wouldn't you say? This revelation was instrumental in reducing my fear of the vast planet. If you go a step further and look at the size of the planet compared with the other planets in our solar system, you will find that we are very small indeed.

So! My perception of the world was inaccurate. It taught me that I could make the world almost any size and the problems any size. How do I do this? Simply by my perceptions, or in other words my thoughts, about things. It was my thinking that was defective.

'What you think about, you bring about.'

James Arthur Ray

I think by now you will see quite clearly how your thinking

about stuff has brought you to your present circumstances. So I needed to change my thinking. I may be repeating myself quite a lot, but this is intentional to continue to stress upon you certain points. And as I stated at the beginning of the book, this is not a literal masterpiece full of large words. This is a tool that will enable those in pain to work through and transform their lives. I have gone out of my way to make this book readable for everyone – an easily understandable and, hopefully, a powerful tool to assist my brothers and sisters who may be in pain right now, to turn their lives around. If I help one, I have accomplished my task. How are you doing? How are things in your life looking now? You can send me the answers to these questions via the internet at: sandy41@blueyonder.co.uk

I have tried to make this book a conversation with you. To be accessible and not just another expert telling you how to change your world. What I am suggesting in this book I have actually applied in my life and in the lives of others with good results. I turned my life from a homeless drunk to one of worth, and one of accepting responsibility for my life, the ups and the downs of it. From being a blight on society to being a contributor to society. I am passionate now about reaching out to my fellow humans who may be at their rock bottom; in their own private hell, not knowing what to do to change things or how to do it.

I have been there. I have not forgotten for a moment the awful emotional turmoil, the sense of defeat, the senseless turmoil, the self-loathing and the utter emptiness of being spiritually dead.

Are these familiar feelings for you? Is this where you are now? The good news is you can turn it around – after all, you created it in the first place, as I did.

Let's get back to the journey. I was asked to treat myself. I did just that, and as I had not been to my town of birth for a very long time I decided to go visit.

I was born in a town called Rosyth in Scotland. I visited my old school and had a look at some of the houses I had lived in.

My mother, bless her, liked to change houses frequently, so I don't think there is an area in Rosyth I have not lived in. My father used to work in the local naval dockyard as a bricklayer. He worked inside boilers relining them with firebricks. His nickname was 'Honest John, the Singing Bricklayer' as he had a good singing voice.

But my sister Jean had a really good operatic voice. She used to play the lead in all the civil service operas. She was a seamstress by trade: a wizard with needle and thread.

My older brother was an officer in the RAF and a fabulous painter. He was very intelligent and moved to New Zealand for a few years. Then he moved again, this time to Australia. He died in

Australia at a young age.

Ian, or Podgy as he was nicknamed, was the next brother to me. He also was very clever and served his apprenticeship as a draughtsman. He died at the age of fifty, which was a very sad family occasion.

And the youngest member is called Roy: nicknamed Butch. He is the only member of our family now living in Scotland.

Out of a family of seven there are only three of us left.

I had a look around the places where I used to play as a child and there were many memories flooding back, I can tell you.

All in all, it was a closure exercise, laying to rest some of the ghosts of the past. I quietly thanked God for my mother and father, my brothers and my sister.

I thanked the God of my understanding for my childhood and all the memories, good and bad. I also thanked God for all my childhood friends.

I did the tourist bit, and looked at my hometown as I had never done before. I was filled with joy seeing the old sights and the changes that had taken place. Some of the old haunts had gone: pulled down to make way for the new buildings.

I suddenly saw quite clearly in my mind's eye, the significance of this visit. This was what I was trying to do with my own life: knock the old thoughts down to make room for the new ones to be built. An internal demolition. Change the thinking that had brought my life to its rock bottom.

One thing was clear: once a building is demolished it is no longer there, except in the mind's eye. You see it all comes back to our thinking. Change the thinking and the heavens will rejoice. This is the whole point of you being where you currently are. The universe has brought you here, not as a form of punishment (although it feels like punishment), but as a chance to change your life, change your circumstances. It's similar, I imagine, to your car finally stopping one metre from the edge of the Grand Canyon. You see your life could be a lot worse if you were to go over the edge and into the Grand Canyon... agreed? Take comfort from this thought.

So what made you reach out for help? Why are you taking the time to read this book? Here is a surprise for you – the reason you are attempting to work the Keys is:

You want to change – and if the ex-tramp writing this book managed to do it, then you sure as hell can also.

And do you know what? You most certainly can, and what's more you will. It is my deepest hope that you are now beginning to see a way out of your present set of circumstances. I rejoice in your success with this programme and so does the God of your own understanding.

The lonely days are over. Being or feeling unloved is also over.

They are in fact a lie. Your higher power has always loved you, but like me you just forgot.

FOOTPRINTS

'One night I had a dream. I dreamed I was walking along the beach with God, and across the sky flashed scenes from my life. For each scene I noticed two sets of footprints in the sand, one belonged to me and the other to God.

When the last scene of my life flashed before us I looked back at the footprints in the sand. I noticed that at times along the path of life there was only one set of footprints. I also noticed that it happened at the very lowest and saddest times of my life.

This really bothered me and I questioned God about it. "God, you said that once I decided to follow you, you would walk with me all the way, but I noticed that during the most troublesome times in my life, there is only one set of footprints. I don't understand why when I needed you most you would leave me."

God replied, "My precious, precious child, I

love you during the most troublesome times in life,
and I would never, never leave you during your
times of trials and suffering. When you see only
one set of footprints it was then I carried you."'

Anon

For me, these words are really beautiful. What do you think? We are moving along now at quite a steady pace; I hope you are still with me. Hang in there – change is on its way.

At this point, it might do a bit of good to review our progress.

We have completed Key One: our life story. Hopefully this has revealed for us the results of incorrect thinking. We have seen how life was, how it has changed and seems to constantly change.

Key Two helped us to admit that there just might be a power greater than us operating in the universe. If that is so, then perhaps this power could help us with our lives. The higher power that you have found is just that: your own understanding.

Key Three helped us to understand the utter importance of applying forgiveness in our own lives and that of others, and how forgiveness ushers in the healing process.

Key Four showed us how the need for change in our life is paramount if we are going to have any success in achieving the life we really want.

So we are slowing turning the Keys that will take us to a new life. A life of love and tenderness; a life of peace and joy. We have a lot of work still to do. But for now take a break; take time out to appreciate who you really are, and who you are becoming. Sit back and close your eyes, now imagine the life that you would like to have. See yourself living this life. What does it feel like? Where are you? Who is with you? What are your surroundings like?

Well, how did doing that exercise feel? I found that it was a very good de-stress exercise. It is one I use quite often. There was an ulterior motive for getting you to try that exercise and we will cover that in length further along.

So now you should be ready to put change into action. Remember there are no grades given for these Keys. They are your Keys to be used in the best way for you. You choose the pace that you undertake them, the pace that suits your needs.

I would say however that the sooner you tackle them the sooner you will get the rewards. And the sooner you will experience the life beyond your wildest dreams.

Your higher power is not going to desert you now. She is ready and willing to help you. This is something you can depend on: a friend who will never let you down, a friend who will never leave you, never abandon you. The one constant in your life. Your job is to ask and God's job is to give. Now that's what I call a deal.

So all in all you have a lot to be grateful for in your life. So let's have a look at the power of gratitude. Let's see what difference is made to your life when you adopt the stance of gratitude.

KEY FIVE

GRATITUDE

KEY FIVE

GRATITUDE

For me this is a very important tool. I make a list, either mentally or written, of all the things I am grateful for in my life every day.

You may be wondering, 'What do I have to be grateful for? My life is a mess.' Well let's see.

Let's talk about me in the hope that it might trigger something in you.

After two months on the streets I wrote my first gratitude list. I imagined that it would be very difficult to accomplish this. I was sitting in my room (that's all I had then) with a notebook and pencil. I wrote at the top of my paper: 'My Gratitude List'. And here it is:

MY GRATITUDE LIST

I am grateful that I am alive.

I am grateful for my body.

I am grateful that I can still use my brain. I can think.

I am grateful that I can see.

I am grateful that I am not deaf.

I am grateful that I can walk.

I am grateful that I have my senses.

I am grateful that I have a bed to sleep in.

I am grateful that I have food to eat.

I am grateful that I have clothes to wear.

I am grateful that I have books to read.

I am grateful I can cry.

I am grateful I can laugh.

I am grateful I can talk.

I am grateful that I am part of the universe.

I am grateful that I AM.

You don't have to reach my rock bottom to suddenly stop taking things for granted. If you are empty, confused, lonely, frightened, angry, desperate and distraught… you are there… this is your rock bottom.

I was pleasantly surprised when I had finished my list. I could see light at the end of the tunnel… yes, I am changing.

It is a great feeling to be able to walk down the street knowing that the nightmare is over; words are inadequate to describe this feeling. The whole world seems different: it seems to be more vibrate, and it's so beautiful to hear the birds singing, to hear the clatter of life all around. But the most important realisation was: 'Hello world, I am Sandy and I am part of the universe… yes sir, I am alive, I AM ALIVE, I AM ALIVE!'

I thank the God of my understanding everyday for every experience that has come my way. I love you, my friend of friends. You have never let me down or left me, and I apologise for doubting you.

So an 'attitude of gratitude' is very important to us if we are to climb out of our current situation. I believe without too much soul searching we will be able to see clearly just how ungrateful we have become.

We blamed our situation on such things as the state of the world, the economic climate, religion, friends, partners, work colleagues and anything else we could think of. From now on we can no longer point the finger at people, places and things, but squarely at ourselves.

We created the mess we find ourselves in. The good news is we are doing something about the situation. We have found true courage, we are looking deeply into ourselves, and we are bent on change. This may appear to be a tall order right now. But with practise it will become easier and easier to maintain an attitude of gratitude, and to your surprise you will wonder how you managed life before without it… the truth is you didn't manage life before, you merely existed. You were just tossed by the winds of fate hither and tether, like an acorn in the Atlantic Ocean. No longer are you a piece of driftwood in the game of life… you are now a player, a full participator. You are a full part of life, a willing member of the human race, you are YOU! How does it feel to be able to stand on your own two feet? I welcome you as my brother or sister and I am proud to walk with you on this journey. You have demonstrated extra-ordinary courage thus far. We will see later how to design the life we have always wanted – that will be fun!

We have had enough misery in our lives… have we not? It's time to declare that we are going to have fun! From now onwards, we are not going to take ourselves so seriously, we are not going to be the centre of the universe.

Remember we are no longer alone. We have a great friend and ally in our higher power. God likes to laugh as well, you know. A God who loves us without reservation or condition, who sees only goodness in all things.

'Reflect upon your present blessings, of which

every man has many; not on your past mis-fortunes, of which all men have some.'

Charles Dickens (1812-1870)

It is my sincere hope that you can understand the paramount importance of an 'attitude of gratitude'. It will make your experience of life much more enjoyable and interesting. And it will make your friends and family view you differently. You will become welcome in their company. You will meet new friends. You will become alive and vibrant. For me, adopting the 'attitude of gratitude' has opened my life up to numerous experiences that before I had only dreamt of.

I am curious about all facets of life and when an offer comes to experience something new I grab it. I am no longer afraid of my shadow. I am no longer afraid of change; nature shows me that change is an important ingredient of life. Therefore to fear change is to fear life. I find myself willing to change, willing to drop outdated attitudes that no longer work for me and step out of my comfort zone once in a while to experience new challenges and meet life on life's terms. To look for the positive in all that happens to me, and not to fling my dummy out the pram every time I do not get what I want. Since I have worked these Keys in my life, I have been catapulted into seventh heaven.

I pray that once we are finished working the Keys this may be your experience.

I have discovered that in truth there are only two true emotions: fear or love – all other emotions come from one or the other. I try to live my life under love. The reasons I do this are many.

One of the reasons is my health. When I live in love I feel good: there is no strain in my life, no stress, no feeling of isolation – all in all a very relaxing way of life. A by-product of trying to live this way is that I have attracted new friends into my life: positive beings who like me are on a spiritual journey. That is the Sixth Key that we will do very shortly. Before this however, I would just like to state something about you:

You are a star glowing in the universe. You are such a glorious child of light and a creature of magnificence. The universe dances to your tune. You are such an amazing person, you are turning into a beautiful butterfly, a unique person, a joy to know and be with. Congratulations child of the universe and welcome to life... I love you.

Do you find that hard to take onboard? I know I did at first. I looked around at the carnage I had created in my life, and wondered who is kidding who here? People know me for the arsehole that I am. They have my number, my card stamped. How do you suddenly accept that you are a beautiful person? I mean, try telling that to the people whose life I have touched. Hey, I am a butterfly. Yippee! Send for the men in the white overalls, he has finally cracked.

Yet the inner me did not seem to have the same problem accepting this as the outer me did. I realised that there were some hidden truths here, and that I would need to at least investigate this more.

Remember: have no contempt prior to investigation.

But where would the starting point be, I wondered? I decided to read all the self-help books I could get my hands on (I recommend that you do the same) looking for clues. Perhaps even a programme that would help me.

What I found most helpful was a scripture in the New Testament:

> *'Unless you are converted and become as little children, you will by no means enter the kingdom of heaven.'*

Matthew 18, Verse 3

It was the words 'little children' that jumped out at me. I suddenly realised that my life story held more clues than I thought. I once again reviewed my story, paying particular attention to my childhood.

This was the starting point for my investigations. It hit me that there were many things that I had not started out to cause. I made a list of things that I had not started out to do or become.

IT WAS NOT MY PLAN TO:

Become a liar.

Become a cheat.

Become a drunk.

Become a drain on society.

Become untrustworthy.

Become a failure.

Become greedy.

Become distrustful.

Become fearful.

And many more things I had not set out to be. You get the idea though. When I was a child I was probably the purest I have ever been. So there was the answer for me. I needed to reclaim what I once was; I needed to get back to my childhood beliefs.

I was happy and free then, my demands on life were minimal

and my attitude was one of joy and excitement.

I remembered that I would spend the whole day climbing trees, imaging I was some great warrior, some hero. I loved jumping in and out of a puddle or riding my imaginary horse. I have actually experienced true happiness, true living and it was as a child. I have simply allowed life to corrupt me, or at least my understanding of life. This seemed to be a great starting point for me to change my life for the better. Or a better way of looking at this was: I am going to reclaim my life. Understanding that at some time in my life I had the ideals that I am now searching for was for me an amazing understanding. I hope you may now better understand the necessity for your life story.

Your own story holds the clues to the answers you are seeking. The reasons why life did not turn out as you had hoped.

You can wallow in self pity when you understand them, or you may choose to learn. I chose to learn from mine. I was aged ten when my emotional growth stopped and when I began constructing the wall. Aged ten! Amazing discovery, don't you think? What happened then, I hear you say? I will share the moment with you, hopefully to help you understand the importance of your childhood and help you to understand yourself a little better. If you can pinpoint the event, you can begin to heal your life.

As I have already told you I was ten years old when this event of monumental significance occurred. My uncle was employed as a chauffeur driver for a racehorse owner and drove a really flash car. I can't exactly remember what type of car, but I think it was a Bentley. He came to visit us because his boss was at the local racetrack running some of his horses. He invited us all to go for a drive in the car (we were all excited about this prospect) but because there was not enough room for all of us my mother said:

'Don't worry about Sandy; he is not bothered with things like that and does not mind not going.'

It was like an electric shock running through my body. I felt left out and not worthy of this trip, and that I was not really wanted. Then I took a deep breath and said, 'OK with me.' I was crying inside and for the first time in my life produced a coat hanger smile. Smiling on the outside, in bits on the inside. This was to become my reaction to the rest of my life... not worthy; nobody really wants me with them. Do you see how events in your own story can help you to understand how you are functioning or not functioning in life today?

In truth I am very grateful that I have managed to discover where my core thinking came from. Now I can change my attitude because I have learned so much from investigating my past. It is the old adage: 'If it isn't bust, don't fix it'. But my attitude was bust and it sure as hell needed fixing. I personally found this exciting.

There was a reason or reasons for my behaviour. There was an answer and there was something I could do about my circumstances.

I really feel quite sorry for my fellow humans who go through life without demonstrating gratitude. You know the sort I am sure: they just take everything for granted. Perhaps this is you? If it is I hope you now can clearly see the need to change this arrogant attitude, can you?

I believe that a person's attitude is paramount to who he is. In my time on this earth I have come across most attitudes. I have experienced for myself the great hurt that some attitudes place on the hearts of the common man. Here are just a few of those negative attitudes – the root of a lot of the world's current ailments.

ARROGANCE

Take pity on the arrogant for their minds are closed, and they will drown in their own superiority. Imagine the closed life they lead and praise the Lord that you do not suffer so.

'He catches the wise in their craftiness'; and again, 'The Lord knows that the thoughts of the wise are futile.'

(1 Corinthians 3:19)

PRIDE

'Pride goes before destruction, and
a haughty spirit before a fall.'

(Proverbs 16:18)

To be filled with pride can sometimes produce very negative results, both in your life and in the world. How often do we see in the news today people being killed in the name of pride? Pride in nations, religions, music and sport – just about any human endeavour. Once it becomes an addiction, we are in serious trouble, whatever the subject may be.

GREED

'... it takes away the life of its owners.'

(Proverbs 1, Verse 19)

Strong words, don't you think? It has been my experience in life that this scripture is very true. Whenever I am coming from the attitude of greed, I become blinded to any principals of goodness, and am probably at my most dangerous. So pride is a 'no-no' for me.

There are of course many more dangerous attitudes to adopt;

the three I have taken time with here are in my opinion the worst for me.

To get our lives back into some sort of order we must avoid negative attitudes wherever possible. Remember we are under new management. The vast majority of the human race do try to lead peaceful lives, and do know right from wrong.

I witnessed an incident today of an Asian woman being arrested in town at the market. What I found abhorrent was the attitude of the arresting officer who was shouting at the lady: 'Why did you come here? What do you want in this country? Why didn't you stay where you were born?' I noticed the people collecting, as they do, to witness the proceedings and nodding their heads in approval. It made me feel quite sick.

So this is why I live my life today in the new spirituality, which basically says we are all one.

Why not take a walk down your local street and really observe what is going on. See the mothers with their children doing the best they can. Notice the old citizen, perhaps walking with sticks, and ask yourself: 'I wonder what events happened in his life – what's his story?' The same for the old lady: what experiences does she have? Once she broke the hearts of young men, once she was in great demand. In short, try walking in other's shoes before you condemn them. What we truly should think when we see people about their business is this: 'I wonder what they have been through in their life? What adventures could they tell I wonder?'

We are all travelling along the same earth and within the same limitations. We are all creating our lives with the tools we have. We are experiencing the joys and the sorrow of life together. As I breathe out so you breathe in. It's the same air, the same moon, the same sun, the same stars, the same atmosphere and hey! That dog you don't like is breathing the same air. What does that tell you?

It told me that we are all one and we truly are all interconnected. If this is true, then why am I fighting life? Why am I sitting in judgement? Or better still, whom am I judging? Myself is the answer.

So, 'gratitude is the attitude'. Heartfelt gratitude is a Key to abundance. It unlocks the great resources of the universe."

Diana cooper

Do you attract air to you to breathe? Or is it just a law? How do we learn to breathe? I can't remember attending class to learn the necessity for breathing, can you? How does the young foal know to stand up as soon as possible? There are laws in the universe and attraction is one of them. Let's now have a look at the Sixth Key.

KEY SIX

✹

ATTRACTION

KEY SIX

ATTRACTION

You have probably heard sayings such as, 'Like attracts like', 'What goes around comes around' and 'You reap what you sow" etc. I know I had heard such sayings all my life, but they were just that: sayings. Probably I used them to sound intelligent!

Out of my studies suddenly came a glaring truth. A moment of inspiration or a moment of universal clarity. One that was sensational and yet very hard to swallow for me and I am guessing it is going to be for you.

The mess my life was in and all the events that I had experienced were OF MY OWN MAKING. I had created all the crap myself. NO! That can't be true, say I!

If it wasn't for this or that or these people or events, my life would be great! After all, who in their right mind would choose alcoholism, homelessness, prison, divorce and bankruptcy as their desire for life? The answer for me: I DID!

It's a hard pill to swallow, I know. But it is one we need to swallow no matter how bitter the taste. Stop reading and think this one out. Your decision can change your life forever.

Once I was able to accept I created my life in every way and orchestrated all the calamities I lost an ally: blame.

I was out of the blame game and left looking in the mirror at the cause of all my downfalls: ME!

My life to date is the result of my thinking. What I think about I create or ATTRACT… attraction!

The significance of accepting you created the mess you find yourself in means that you can from this MOMENT recreate your life with the outcomes you desire. For the first time probably in your life you are not asleep. You are finally responsible for your life and you are in control. You have the most under-used power in the universe – the God of your understanding – with you. You are no longer alone, *not that you ever were.* Now it is up to you! This is why it was necessary to write your life story. To find out how your life turned out when you were in charge. Enough said, I think. You get the picture.

So remember, 'What you think about you bring about.' Stick that statement all around the house, on the mirrors, on the fridge etc. It's never easy to master new tools – that is why carpenters serve apprenticeships. You will constantly forget to use your new tools… don't beat yourself up when you do! Remember you are modelling your life in a new way. You are taking responsibility for yourself. And that will take time. So I had to become totally aware of my thoughts, and I had to become an observer of my thinking. Whenever negative thoughts were present I had to replace them with positive thoughts and to continue to be on guard. This you will have to do also. To say it will be easy would be to dismiss all that has happened in your life to this moment. Your mind thinks that it is in charge and will not let go of this feeling of importance easily, but you can and will train your mind to think in a completely different manner: a positive and life transforming manner.

How do you do this, I hear you say? Well, you have to input new programming into your mind. This is how I did it and it worked for me and has also worked for the people whose lives I have been blessed to help change for the better.

I wrote a list of positive stuff about me and repeated it last thing at night and first thing in the morning, and also throughout the day if I was feeling negative. I still do this to this day. So here is my list. You of course can compile your own to suit your own circumstances. I hope you are still with me and that you are doing the work required in an absolutely honest way. Only if you are honest with yourself will any of this work. So stop and ask yourself this question: 'Am I really being honest with myself?' If the answer is yes, here is my list:

I am an amazing human being.

I am happy.

I am love.

I am kindness.

I am truth.

I am successful.

I am abundance.

I am compassionate.

I am healthy.

I am one with the universe.

From this day forth I will feed my mind with loving thoughts. Yesterday is gone and tomorrow is out of sight.

Today is all there is. Therefore my reality is in this day. Today I will be the most amazingly loving person I can be. I can do this for a day. And guess what? The days become weeks, the weeks months and the months years. You can do it! I know you can and thank God YOU know you can.

I wish you all that you wish yourself. Start to keep a diary or a written log of your day.

Ask yourself, 'What do I want?' Then tell the universe what you want. The universe will rearrange things to achieve what you desire. You are now the master of your life and your desires. Nothing is impossible for you to achieve, child of the universe.

Sing! Shout! Dance! You are free! At last you are a free spirit. Life awaits your wishes and dreams, like a giant supermarket.

Place your order and stand back and watch the miracle that is life transform you.

Be awake: the universe speaks in many ways and takes many forms – perhaps the next tune you hear, the next person you meet, the next word you read, the next smell, the next thought, the next tree you see, the next flower you see, the next poem you read… get the picture?

'I am with you always and in all ways.'

Neale Donald Walsch, Conversations with God, *Book I*

I am going to offer help via the internet to those who need it; I will leave details at the end of this book. I hope by now you are going with the flow – sensing that divine power moving you along life's journey with a sense of purpose and direction.

Gone now is that fear of being alone, unloved, uncared for, rejected, unworthy, undeserving and all the rest of the lies we told ourselves through the years.

Now comes an astounding fact: do not think of wanting things such as 'I want to be rich' or 'I want to be successful'. All you will experience is the feeling of wanting. Instead, be grateful for what you have and thank the universe for the abundance it has sent you. Live your life in an abundant way and the universe will manifest abundance as your experience.

Live abundantly! What are you talking about, I am broke! If this is your thinking, you are making the most common error regarding abundance. Abundance is only money. This is not true. I dare you to visit your local hospital for a day. Look around, talk to some of the patients.

I guarantee that when you leave the hospital you will know how abundant you are. Can you help the hospital? Can you give some time to taking the patients for a walk or perhaps reading them a story? Do this and your heart will overflow with gratitude. Trust me, you will feel like a millionaire.

I mentioned the word 'broke', and you, like I used to, immediately thought of money. You are not broke. You have talent, you care about things. You are a being of love – you have just forgotten. The world needs you! If you are still reading this book and doing the work, you are a great person and a real blessing to the world. You can make a difference to how things are. Look at the world – what do you like? What do you not like?

You can begin to change the world, but first you need to change you. I applaud your courage in doing that.

KEY SEVEN

DESIGN YOUR LIFE

KEY SEVEN

DESIGN YOUR LIFE

Time for a review of our progress thus far. By now you should have your life story, found a higher power, forgiven, changed and been introduced to the laws of attraction. These are necessary Keys to begin to design your new life.

How then do you set about designing your new life? By looking at your life story and being certain about what you don't want. It's time now to let go of that old life – the one that never worked for you – and to declare what your new life is going to be like.

This is the fun part of the Keys. You should by now have done the required work to establish what you don't want to see in your life anymore.

> *'We are co-creators with God, not puppets*
> *on a string waiting for something to happen.'*
>
> *Leo Booth*

What an amazing statement... don't you think? I certainly do.

It is quoted to remind you that you are now no longer alone in designing your life. You need not carry the full burden; you can share it with your creator. Have fun with your higher power for He will never let you down. She will always be with you, at all times and in all events.

OK, time to do some more work – fun work this time. It is time to dream and dream big. How would you like your world to be? Now is your chance to vision the best for you… oops! Stop.

Give yourself permission to dream. Say it is OK to dream… this is the beginning of your new creation. This is your precious time with your higher power. You are in for a universal treat and you deserve this.

YOU DESERVE THIS TIME.

OK, let's go. Sit yourself in your comfy seat. Turn the phone off and the mobile. Light a candle and burn an incense stick. Have loose fitting clothing or better still none. Allow yourself say a half hour, or any length of time you are comfortable with. Firstly breathe deeply and slowly.

Say hello to your body. Feel your body in your mind, feel your face, your smile, your neck, shoulders, your arms, your fingers, chest, torso, legs, feet and toes. Thank your body for bringing you this far, and say: 'I love you'.

Let your mind wander. Let your mind show you things. Now picture yourself three months from now – what are you doing? Who is with you? If you see nothing then visualise what you want your life to be like in three months. Be specific about this. Picture the people, the place and the situation you want in three months.

Go on! It's your creation, subject only to your own self-imposed limitations.

How much money would you like to have in three months? Be specific! See your bank statement with that amount on it. Who would you like to have in your life in three months? What would you like to be doing in three months time?

If you can see it, you can create it.

Remember the universe will do everything to help you create your dream.... everything. Have fun – it's your moment, it's your creation; this is who you are going to be... no doubts.

Your higher power has not brought you this far to simply abandon you at this moment of creation... the heavens are dancing to your tune. Life is exited, are you? Get excited! Get excited!

Put your emotions behind this moment, feel it and own it... it is yours. What you can see is yours...

Have some fun and extend the limits of possibilities for yourself. Be brave and be creative. Have a go.

Well done my friend. Now come back to your environment and write down in your log or diary all the events you want to happen in three months. If you visualised anything, write it down.

This is the procedure you use to slot things into your life. Your life is no longer subject to flights of fancy. No sir! You are in charge. You are the creator of your life. You now decide how you want your life to be. And that is a blessing from the universe to you.

The sky is the limit. You can go six months or six years into the future, putting in place what you want your life to be at that point.

There are no restrictions on how you can design your life, except the ones you put in place yourself.

I understand that all this may seem daunting to you, and the temptation to quit before you really try may seem the better or easier option. A timely reminder may be needed here. You bought this book because your life was in a mess, or at the very least miserable and unfulfilled. Why else? So keep on! Don't quit now. The very change you seek might just be around the corner, about to bloom. The Keys are not easy, but they are rewarding.

So! Keep on trying. The rewards far outweigh the effort, and you only have to do this once. If like me you have messed your life up, probably causing chaos among your family, friends and society in general, then the effort is surely the least you can do to end the chaos.

Imagine your life as it can be, not as it has been: you are indeed a child of God and worth more. The only reason for me to write this book was to give back what I have received, to offer hope to my fellow sufferer and to lift you up as I was lifted up by my coaches.

So at this point let me applaud your courage to change and your willingness to try something new. I am with you every step of the way; you are such a special person.

Hey! If a drunken homeless tramp can do it, so can you.

You are surely going to have off days: times when you wonder if you are not simply kidding yourself. I certainly had these days, but I had to get back in touch with the God of my understanding and ask for help.

There are many obstacles put in your way, and most of the time they come from well-meaning friends or family members. You have to declare over and over to yourself who you now want to be, and what kind of person you want to be.

Like anything that is new, the more you do it the easier it becomes, or as some would say: practise makes perfection. But you are no longer alone in your life. You have a power greater than you to guide you – all you have to do is sincerely ask for help and you will receive it.

> *'Ask and it will be given to you; seek and you will find; knock and it will be opened to you.'*
>
> *(Matthew 7, Verse 7)*

So you see it is a promise from your higher power. You can

read these promises all day long but if you do not believe them in your heart nothing will work. The biggest stumbling block to designing your life is fear. Let's have a look at fear and see if we can better understand this emotion.

FEAR

There are many books written about this emotion. As I have clearly stated, this book is not a literal masterpiece – nor is it meant to be. I am only interested in getting the message over clearly, so that you can start to change your unsatisfied life to one of satisfaction.

BIRTH

This is going to be our starting point because we are not born in fear; you only have to look at a newborn child to see this. We are born unable to speak and when you think about it there is no real reason why this should be so. It is well known that we are able to hear in the womb, so why are we born unable to speak? It is my belief that our early existence is a process of forgetting: forgetting the glory from which we have come from to this life on earth. The closest you can ever be to true love is in the actions of a baby. It would be true to say that we are fearless as a baby, so where does fear come from? If we were born fearless then it must be equally true that we had to learn to fear. So the question surely is how do we learn fear? The answer brings us back to the cause of our pain and that is our mind. What goes on between the ears determines how our life is lived out.

What we think about, we bring about.

Probably the best way to understand this is to give an example of the fear process. It is simplified for this illustration, but the point will be clear.

Fear components consist entirely of your mind; your thinking process. Behind the mind lies consciousness. Consciousness does not need the mind, but the mind needs consciousness to feed it images and information. So all that chitter-chatter that goes on in your mind is the mind trying to exert its importance upon you. When you are asleep your consciousness can function perfectly well, hence dreams.

The mind can only function on information from the consciousness.

So as a baby when you become hungry you make it perfectly clear what you want by yelling, screaming and crying. The parent rushes in and feeds you. Aha! You think: yell and scream and I will get what I want. So a simple script is put in place – this action produces the desired result, and so it is stored in the consciousness. However, the downside to this action is that sooner or later you will not get the desired outcome and you will begin to feel abandoned and begin to panic and introduce the emotion of fear – fear of abandonment. Fear is a most uncomfortable feeling, and one you must do everything you can not to experience, so you begin to adopt new actions. Perhaps you yell louder or scream louder or throw everything out of the pram. No matter what you do, you have experienced this terrible emotion known as fear, and it will stay with you the rest of your life.

This is a very basic example, but I use it to simply illustrate that we learn fear. But here is an interesting bit of information: because you reacted in a certain way to a set of circumstances you also began building your personality. But also take note that the pure, loving innocence you had as a baby, the real you, is still the same deep inside – in the place some call the soul.

Now of course your mind is taking over and controlling how you will feel about any given set of circumstances. How does the mind do this? Simple by collecting images and past experiences from the subconscious, and based on how you reacted probably years ago, decides that in this given situation you should feel such and such, and what you know you do.

Whether you believe Hitler is dead or not will not alter the fact that he is dead. Do you see? That fact is simply a fact. The feelings, however, are what you have imagined. So keeping it simple, the experiences you have had up until now, and the emotions applied to them, have formed your personality and determined who you are.

By the same token you could just as easily say that your external affairs have formed your personality. However, your true internal condition is one of love and joy. We have lost contact with our true natures – probably due to the external clamour of living, or what we think is living. Remember that when we die we take nothing with us and that is an undisputable fact. We are all caught up in a lie – that is the truth; we are all rushing around like headless chickens getting nowhere fast. Why? Because this is what we have been taught from a very early age

'You have no right to be unhap-
py ever, because life is good.'

'There is no unhappiness in events.'

'You are not just living, you are life.'

'Surrender is now and you are free.'

'Unhappiness is substantial.'

(Some quotations from Only Fear Dies, by Barry Long)

I don't know how old you are, dear reader. You may be in your teens, middle-aged or elderly, but it does not matter in the least how old you are. Why? Because in absolute truth all we really have is now – this moment, this day.

The plus side to this understanding is that we truly can choose who we want to be from this moment. We can act out the kind of person we would wish to be now. We do not have to wait a required amount of time – we can do it now.

Life will not let you down. People will, but life will not. I think we would all have to agree that life is all around us. Whether we drop down dead or not will make no difference to life – it goes on and on, dare we be brave enough to say, eternally. Now change the word life, replace it with God and we have perhaps a better under-standing of God.

As I have stated previously I have been on a spiritual quest for over thirty years. I have yearned to get close to the God of my own understanding, and I am pleased to announce I have finally reached that starting point in my life. It is a fantastic place to be. My life today is beyond my wildest dreams and that is why I am talking to you: I want to share my joy with you. The Keys are the tools to uncover the hidden you, the real you. They will help you put all pretence down, finally drop the mask of fear and to replace it with the face of the real you: a beautiful person, perfect in the eyes of your higher power and a person in which God could truly say:

'This is my beloved in whom I am well pleased.'

This is a better condition than the one you were in when you first began reading this book, is it not?

It is break time. Time to treat yourself to that something a little special just for you. Come on, get on with it.

Welcome back. Well? We have touched a little on the power of fear. You will need to start looking for the books that uplift you. Try spiritual bookshops and make it a priority to find the books you need to help you along. At the end of this book I will give you some recommended reading to help you along.

You need to replace all the negativity in your life with positive stuff that is the proper food for your spiritual journey. You are now responsible for you and you can create the life you want. You are under new management.

So my friend, the journey begins. I think you are a champ to have come so far... well done.

KEY EIGHT

THE JOURNEY BEGINS

KEY EIGHT

THE JOURNEY BEGINS

The journey begins – your journey begins. By now you should have found out a lot out about yourself. You now should know what you like about you and what you don't like about you. You should have a good idea what you want from your life and what you no longer want in your life.

So as you start to walk as the new you it is wise to remember that you are no longer alone on your journey. You have constant help available from your higher power: all you have to do is ask.

Like all journeys you need a map or directions to get you to your destiny. We are going to discuss now just such a map or formula for achieving the best you can in your life. This will take you to the next grander level of who you are and all you can become.

The carnage of your past life may be ever present and, if you allow it, threatening you with impending doom. But you are no longer adopting the ostrich stance, head-in-the-sand, no sir! So we need to tidy up our affairs, wouldn't you agree?

In my experience our maladies fall into three categories: financial, emotional and spiritual, is this not so?

So let's have a look at our financial state. Let's try and reduce the monster to a manageable size.

FINANCES

As you can probably understand my finances were in a terrible state when I reached my rock bottom. I owed thousands so I do understand just how daunting that can feel, and if you let it, it can be very crippling. I was very lucky. I had a wise old man to help me in sorting out my finances, and this is what he told me, and what I acted on, to reduce the monster to a pussycat.

STEP 1

Write down my total income on a sheet of A4. Then add up my outgoings, rent, heating, electric, gas, telephone (yes, telephone – you do not want to end up isolated because you cannot make contact with people), food, clothing allowance and a couple of pounds spending money.

STEP 2

Subtract the outgoings from your income and you are left with the amount you can use to get out of debt. Now let us suppose you owe 10 debtors x amount of money. You simply divide the amount you have for paying off your debts by ten. The sum you arrive at is the sum you can pay weekly or monthly to each of your creditors.

STEP 3

Write ten letters, one for each creditor, explaining your financial position and offering them the amount that you have come to. And that is that. All of a sudden you hopefully have reduced the monster financial mess to a manageable set of accounts. You are in charge of your life, not the debtors, and you have taken the necessary steps to achieve this.

EMOTIONAL

If only emotional issues were as easy to sort out as your finances. Afraid not. The advice I was given was to put these issues on hold and to concentrate on sorting myself out by working the Keys to discovery.

Remember the mess you have got yourself in is only a symptom of a deeper underlying problem. We need to work on that problem within us before we try to change the world. All this might be beginning to sound rather difficult, but I assure you, if you do the Keys honestly and properly you will empower yourself to deal with the emotional issues in your life.

However there are some among you who may need professional help to overcome your emotional problems, and that is perfectly OK. Use professional people when you can to assist you in any problems you may have: financial, emotional or spiritual.

SPIRITUAL

When someone first told me I was spiritually sick, I had not a clue what they were talking about. My head was off on one:

> *What do they mean? Religion, Christianity... what are they talking about?*

But my true condition was that I was dead inside. I had a numb feeling that was overwhelming me. A blackness of the soul is what people mean by spiritually bankrupt, yes sir – I was spiritually dead. I had no hope, nothing to look forward to except death, which, at that time, I would have welcomed. It feels strange for me to talk like that now, but that was my condition at that time. And if it is yours please believe me when I tell you that it will change. I am not talking to you out of some theory: I am talking to you out of my truth, my experiences. What I was like and what I am like now.

So I say to you no matter how far down you may have gone, you can change everything around. I would say that emotional and spiritual matters are ongoing and we deal with them one day at a time. The spiritual part of my life – no! That's not expressing it correctly. My spiritual life is becoming stronger each day and it is so wonderful to know that I am truly loved, warts and all, by my higher power. There is nothing I have to do to please the God of my understanding but be myself. Did you hear that? Just be myself. I think that is great. What about you?

So we do have to address the carnage of the past, but that is no reason to stop growing or living. A saying that I was given and that I now pass to you really helped me:

Give time time.

Well, how do you start your journey? What do we need to do? Is there a blueprint we can use to start the process of empowerment? In short, yes. There are certain things that we can do now to start our journey. Firstly we need discipline to start to run our lives on a different schedule. All I can do here is to tell you what I did, in the hope that it may help you.

OUR TIME

First thing in the morning I have a quiet time – a time just to sit and be still and to listen to my inner voice. A time to connect with my higher power and to thank Her for another amazing day.

Then I read my daily reading from *Until Today* by Iyanla Vanzant.

I would highly recommend this book to you. The book is set out for daily readings and does help me to connect with my God. Often I read the daily reading a couple of times. I find that it helps to empower me for the day.

THINGS TO DO

I have a cuppa and sit down to write my list of things to do today. The reason I do this is simply to apply discipline and structure to my life.

SHOUT HELLO

Sounds silly I know, but I always shout hello to the world and thank you God for a brand new day. You're ready then to meet life on life's terms.

I of course have no way of knowing individual circumstance. Some of you may be working, others may be ill and yet others might not have a job.

But to those of you who have time on your hands I would like to share with you what I did with my time. I didn't have a job when I started attempting to change my life; the truth is I was unemployable.

I found that time weighed quite heavily on me, and it was always dangerous to be left in my head. So I took to structuring my day, and there is no doubt that a structured life is the best.

In the morning, regardless of the weather, I would go out for a walk, meditating on my daily reading as I went along.

I'd come back and make myself a lunch, then do some reading for an hour or so, then begin to make a list of all the people my previous attitude had hurt. I promised myself that when the time was right and I was spiritually stronger I would apologise to those people.

I also looked around the community to see if I could do some voluntary work. It was my idea of putting or giving something back to the community, and I managed to get myself a job as a befriender in a drop-in centre. This was great, as I got to meet all kinds of people with various social and mental problems, and strange as it may seem I began to feel clean from the inside – a great feeling.

I would get home and make myself a meal, then sit down and listen to music (all New Age relaxing music) I had discovered.

I would often meet up with friends that I had met during the day for a cup of coffee and a chat.

I would have a bath and really pamper myself with scented water and just relax and be grateful that I had somewhere to live, new friends and a fabulous higher power. I was still up to my ears in debt, but miracle of miracles, I was building a new life – one of honour and decency – and that felt just great.

God's miracle was unfolding on a daily basis for me, and it will for you – provided you have done the required work using the Keys.

Your world is at your feet: go out and get it – you deserve a good life, as does everyone else.

'Life will work for me when I re-alise I must put first things first.'

'Life will work for me when I realise I must make myself available to life.'

'Life will work for me when I realise I have the power to walk right! The power to talk right! And the peace to live right.'

'Life will work for me when I realise that try-
ing to prove something to someone is nev-
er a valid reason for doing anything.'

Some daily headings from Until Today *by Iylanla Vanzant*

Now perhaps you see the value of getting a copy of this book. Believe me when I tell you that when you sincerely try to live a spiritual life, you will be amazed by what transpires in your life. For me it unfolded like a magic carpet. I went directions I had never, ever thought about before, and here I am sitting at my computer writing a book. If that is not an example of a miracle I don't know what is. Do you?

If you found Aladdin's lamp, rubbed it and the genie appeared asking for your three wishes, what would you wish? Write down your three wishes, put them in an envelope, seal the envelope and have a look in about six months and see how your three wishes may now change.

Another very important tool for your journey is a diary or journal. You need to keep a record of your feelings and what you did that day. The purpose of this is twofold: firstly it disciplines you to begin to take responsibility for your life and secondly you can see your progress at any given time so it will help you to be truly grateful for your life.

Gone are the hip hap days of bygone years. Now you and your

higher power are in control of your life. You are no longer adrift on the sea of life; you are each day involved in the creation of your life.

You make decisions about your life to encompass what you want out of it, and negativity no longer has room in your life. Tell me you don't feel good about that – how could you not feel excited about all the possibilities before you? You have resurrected that most wonderful of feelings: the feeling of hope. That in itself is a miracle.

As a child, what sports or hobbies did you enjoy? What got you excited? Well perhaps it's time to rekindle lost interests. Or it may be time to look at things you at one time had hoped to do in your life (maybe to fly for example), and aim for it now. Take some time to have a real hard look at all the things you had hoped to experience in your life, and plan to start achieving those experiences now. There is no limit to what you are able to achieve now that you are under new management. Is there?

It is the time now to be very grateful and to start to enjoy your life to the full. What has happened in your life has happened – there is no way you can go back in time to make it better; this is something you are just going to have to accept. You can, however, make amends to you and others by not repeating old behaviour, by holding your head up high, looking people squarely in the eye and adopting new behaviours such as gentleness, honesty and helpfulness. Appreciate what you have got as opposed to moaning about what you do not have. There are many positive and very rewarding attitudes that you can adopt as of now. They do not depend upon your circumstances, whether you are rich or poor, because in your life now if you adopt these principals you are a millionaire.

Do you see this? Can you understand this? It's true you have come from despair to hope. When you started this book there seemed no way out of your current situation did there? Now look at you!

I hope that by now you can see some light at the end of the tunnel, and that you have hope for your future. Let's now take a look at the last Key.

KEY NINE

24 HOURS IS A LIFETIME

KEY NINE

24 HOURS IS A LIFETIME

'Therefore do not worry about tomorrow, for tomorrow will worry about its own things. Sufficient for the day is its own troubles.'

Matthew 6, Verse 34

That scripture is quite clear about living in the day. It talks about sufficiency for the day. We are therefore given enough strength to get through the day, and to meet all the challenges we may face.

For the sake of argument and to make a point, let's imagine that the strength we are given for the day is a unit of ten. So we start our day with sufficient strength: ten. But what happens if we start to relive the past? By reliving a past scenario, or simply wallowing in self pity of what might have been, we are using up three of our daily strength units. Oops! Now we are living our day on seven units.

Equally draining is worrying about what might happen in the future, so we spend energy fretting about what the future may hold for us – another three units of energy wasted. Oops! Now we are functioning on only four units of the energy we were given for our day.

Now little daily problems start to become monumental Why? Because we are depleted in energy. We do not have enough energy for the day, so a cycle has begun. We almost certainly end up having a stressful and irritable day. And it is ourselves to blame for this; no one else is responsible for our day but us.

So the trick is to stop wasting our energy supply on yesterday or tomorrow, but to stay focused on the day. 24 hours is a lifetime.

'Thinking of the past or future only
arises from unhappiness.'

Barry Long

So there you have it, summed up for us in a simple statement. To understand, just recall a time when you were really enjoying yourself. You never gave a thought to yesterday or tomorrow, you were in the day, in the moment, in the now. Therein lies a great secret: contain yourself within the lifetime of 24 hours. In reality that is all you have. Only your higher power knows what this day will bring. Is it to be your last?

What if it was to be your last! Would you continue not to speak to your loved ones because they hurt your pride? Would you sit at home feeling sorry for yourself? Would you perhaps stay in bed hiding? Would you put off doing that adventure that you had promised to do one day? I think not.

I for one would be out there doing all the things I want to do, making peace with the world, and myself, with a sense of urgency. What about you?

It never ceases to amaze me how my life changes when I have a change in my perception of what is for me.

PERCEPTION

'Everything you see or hear or experience in any way at all is specific to you. You create a universe by perceiving it, so everything in the universe you perceive is specific to you.'

Douglas Adams, Mostly Harmless

It is strange to think that no two people ever see an object the same. They may have an overall agreement on their perception in general, but not in the fine details. There is something we see in every object that is special to us.

An example of what I am saying here may be that you and I are sitting watching a beautiful sunset together. We may both agree that it was pretty spectacular, but it was unique for you because you noticed the flock of birds and missed what made it unique for me: the North Star rising. Do you see what I mean now? Overall we agreed, but individually it was unique to you and I.

So it is true to say that we all may look similar, but we are individually unique. No two persons are the same, hence our unique fingerprints and DNA. I believe this was a grave error in my judgement in the past: assuming that everyone knew what I meant or how I felt. Now today I understand the folly of such thinking, and just how ridiculous such an assumption is.

Like you, I am learning every day how to live a life of worth to me, and how to give something back to the world – something that may benefit others, as I have truly benefited from others who gave of their time for me. For me today, it is about what can I do to be of service to my fellows.

SERVICE

I look upon service as simply being available at all times to respond to my inner voice, or to reach out and talk to that stranger at the coffee bar, just to say hello. There is no such thing in life as coincidence – more like God-incident. Do not let the opportunity pass you by, for you may have missed the opportunity to speak to an Angel.

I have learned a great deal about myself through talking to you, and through sharing some of my experiences. I have relived many of my own nightmares, and for me this has also been, to a certain degree, a validation of how well I am doing today in my own life.

So I highly recommend, if you can, that you make yourself available to be of service to the universe, so that you do not miss that opportunity, or God-incidence.

'What you do for another, you do for yourself.'

From Conversations With God, *by Neale Donald Walsch*

'The universe loves you and holds a vision of your future as an enlightened person no matter what mistakes you are making on earth.'

'The universe waits without judgement as we experience and learn. When we are ready it opens new doors.'

Diana Cooper, A Little Light on the Spiritual Laws

Another favourite saying that I like is: 'When the pupil is ready the teacher will come'. I think this saying is of eastern origin.

We are all on a journey, some are awake, others are asleep, some are blind, others are deaf. Regardless of a human's personal condition they are still on a journey. Now it is my hope that you are awake for the rest of your journey, that you are more tolerant of the less fortunate, more compassionate towards your fellow travellers, more understanding, more helpful and no longer feel that you are the centre of the universe. So you are now beginning the longest journey of all – a journey into the self and I applaud you.

So if you have found this book helpful then please drop me a line at sandy41@blueyonder.co.uk. On the other hand, if you found it to be load of rubbish still contact me.

REMEMBER:

What you say about another is a reflec-
tion of what is going on inside of you.

LIFE STORY

It is more important that you know yourself inti-
mately. Then and only then you may know others.

HIGHER POWER

My job is to give you what you
ask: your job is to ask.

FORGIVENESS

To err is human, to forgive is divine.

CHANGE

All seasons change. They come
and go; as does all life.

GRATITUDE

Heartfelt gratitude is a Key to abundance.

ATTRACTION

You are a magnet: you attract like to you.

DESIGN

What you think about, you bring about.

JOURNEY

The cycle of life is your individual journey.

24 HOURS

All you really have is the now.

EXAMPLES OF HOW TO USE THE NINE KEYS IN EVERY-DAY LIVING

It is one thing to say that working the Nine Keys will transform your life, and quite another to truly believe that they will. For this reason I have decided with the approval of four former clients (who are now friends) to illustrate further the dramatic affect that working the Nine Keys will have on your life. In my career to date I have had the pleasure of working with a very wide section of society, from down-and-outs to millionaires, and they all have one thing in common: they are all victims to some degree of the cancerous emotion – FEAR.

So no matter what your present condition may be, if you are not happy with how you feel, you can change and change quickly. We are not on this planet to suffer – that is contrary to our inner natures. We are here to create joy, love and harmony and to contribute in some way to the planet – to make a difference if you will.

I have changed the name, age and location of my clients, but the actual case studies are accurate. I hope to be able to demonstrate that this programme is for everyone regardless of his or her current status.

It can be used to deal with addictions, money matters, relationships and lack of direction, or simply to increase your abundance. We can and will all benefit from having a closer look at our lives.

I always tell my clients that you have to empty out the rubbish from yourselves in order to be able to incorporate positive life-changing material. We live in extraordinary times. We have the internet, mobile phones, television, video players, MP3 players, satellite guidance, cinema, etc. You get the picture!

If our life at the moment is not a happy one all the above-mentioned wonders are nothing but a distraction. It has the same action as medication in that it eases the pain but does not address the underlying issues that are causing the disease. Can you see that? Do you understand this?

It never ceases to amaze me that when I ask people that I meet:

'How are you?', 99% will answer: " I am fine!" – even though I know for sure that they are not. What's that all about? Let me tell you. We are being brought up to believe in a stiff upper lip, big boys don't cry... no! They just die!

Wipe that smirk off your face or I will wipe it off for you.

Wear clean underwear in case you are run over by a bus.

What ever happens in the house stays in the house.

Life is a struggle, etc. etc. etc.

You have my full permission to cry if you want to, smile if you want to, sing if you want to, daydream if you want to, talk to anyone you want to and be with anyone you want to. Now here is the trick: you need to give yourself permission to do just that. Let's talk, for God's sake, let's talk to one another, let's smile at each other, let's be gentle with each other – why? Because every single soul on the planet has the same desire you have! To love and be loved – that's it, pure and simple.

It was about four years ago that I first met Liz; she was recommended to me by one of her friends. I remember with great clarity our first meeting. She arrived at 10am wearing all black and with a face to match. She was carrying the problems of the world on her shoulders. Here is some of the dialogue we exchanged:

Liz: I don't know what I'm doing here.

Me: Oh really! Well come back when you do know.

Liz: What do you mean by that?

Me: Simple. If you do not know what you are doing here, we have nothing to work with.

Liz: I was told you could help me.

Me: I can! But you don't know what you are doing here!

Liz: I am hurting, I am in pain, my life is a mess, I want to cry but I can't, nothing is working for me in life (the tears streamed down her face as she was speaking).

I was immediately filled with love and compassion for this human being. She exposed her vulnerability and she looked like an angel. I clearly saw the presence of God in her, and I knew that we could work together, that we could learn from each other and that we could grow together.

Any so called expert who sees you as the patient has learned all he or she knows from a set of books, and this can be more damaging than good. I can and do state this, as it is my experience.

The Beatles had it right when they sang: 'All You Need is Love'.

I detest any form of bullying masquerading as 'good for you', 'we have only your best interests at heart' and so on. People who say this are under the full control of their God: fear. They have set themselves up in an ivory tower, full of their own importance.

Anyhow, back to Liz. We agreed that she would write her own life story (Key One) and we'd meet again in two weeks time.

Liz arrived for our second session looking a lot less burdened, but still wore a drab-coloured outfit.

This is what is discovered from Key One. She uncovered sexual abuse in her childhood (everything that happens in the house stays in the house), and there was a put down awaiting her every time she tried to do something that she wanted to do. She remembered being pulled to the side by one of her teachers and told she was scruffy. All in all she uncovered nine situations in her life that were cruel and soul destroying. They were in fact the triggers that would affect how she would handle situations for the rest of her life. Incidentally, Liz was not addicted to any chemical substance and had never indulged in any mood altering substance.

It was a really moving session and I could see the strain fall from her face and she began to smile. It was like the sun coming out from behind a cloud. She lit up the room.

Upon writing up my case notes I could not help but be struck by her honesty and her inner warmth. We agreed to crack on with Key Two, and arranged to meet in a week's time at the local Abbey. The grounds of the Abbey are really staggeringly beautiful and oh so serene. A place where one could be at ease and just enjoy the scene.

God was smiling on us when we met at the Abbey gardens. The sky was blue, the sun was shining and so was Liz.

She was beginning to look a different person and she was dressed like a rainbow. She had reconnected with the God of her own understanding. We had a great time together, like two school kids on a day out. Liz worked through the rest of the Keys very rapidly and it has to be said, with great enthusiasm.

The working of the Keys gave her direction in life. Liz now knew what she wanted to do with the rest of her life. She has moved from a life of fear and darkness to one of light, hope and joy. She is now a successful set designer. Everyday she wakes up with excitement and love for the new day. She said to me only last week that her life is beyond her wildest dreams. I now refer to her as 'Miss Dynamite'. We have become firm friends. She is hoping to get married next year.

So you see the new Keys will benefit everyone who has the courage to try them, and unless and until you try them you will never know. Will you?

How can the Nine Keys help a millionaire? A man who has everything: a yacht, houses all over the world and a thriving business. Well believe it or not they can, and in the case of Ian they did. Ian was recommended by one of his friends to come and have a chat with me. So out of the blue I received a call from Ian asking to meet with me for a chat. I agreed and we arranged a meeting.

When I first met Ian he certainly looked the part, dressed in designer clothes and draped in gold. His demeanour was that of a not too happy bunny. His defence for this was to be boisterous, and to demonstrate an attitude of self-reliance. Ian's initial problem was centred on relationships with the opposite sex. He had been married twice and had been in many relationship that all ended messily.

So I agreed to help him work through the Nine Keys. After his life story he was absolutely blown away when he saw and recognised for the first time where his problems lay. He could not stop talking – he was so excited.

He continued through the Nine Keys and came out the other side a more gentle and loving man – a man who was fun to be with, a man who stopped making demands on his nearest and dearest and finally accepted the slogan:

Live and let live.

When I reflect on this case it never ceases to amaze me how in today's world we do not feel comfortable really telling people how we feel, what we fear, what we want for ourselves and how we would like our life to be. Here was a man who appeared to have his life together, appeared to want for nothing and yet deep inside was very lonely.

For those who may be struggling with relationships, try the Nine Keys. You have nothing to lose and perhaps all to gain. When you have finished the Nine Keys I highly recommend you read:

The Road Less Travelled

By M. Scott Peck

Conversations with God

By Neale Donald Walsch

I suppose it would be true to say that I have had the pleasure of working with about 200 people over the last twenty years or so and to help them to help themselves. It is very rewarding for me and quite frankly I look upon it as a gift from the God of my understanding. For that gift I am truly grateful.

I am still in contact with Ian and he is doing even better in his business than he did before – his colleagues are utterly amazed at his turn around.

So there you have it. I think this case clearly demonstrates the programme is for everybody no matter what your circumstance may be at this present time. I have no doubt in my mind whatsoever that my God put this together as a tool to help thousands of people, and to assist them in understanding themselves and to grow and evolve. My input was simply to have the courage to expose all my defects honestly and openly with you. This I have done.

The third person I would like to introduce to you is John, an outspoken, aggressive Glaswegian. The original mister angry, there was nothing that he did not know about – a real barrack-room lawyer. He was currently 'in between jobs', as he put it. I was reluctant to take him on. I am what is known in Britain as a senior citizen and I do not charge any money as I am on state pension. The question that I had to ask myself was, 'Do I need the aggravation that may result with John?' After thinking about this matter very thoroughly I decided to at least meet John face to face and to be guided in my decision making process by my intuition. I arranged to meet John in a public place – a café that I am rather fond of and visit most mornings to meet up with friends.

Checking out my feelings as I drove to meet John I had to acknowledge a certain amount of trepidation. What is John going to be like? What if he starts bawling and shouting? What if he turns violent? So for me it was a challenge just to make the appointment. Soon my fears were allayed, as he was already sitting there with a coffee as peaceful as you like. I could see that he had made an effort to spruce himself up; this impressed me. He offered to buy me a coffee; I politely declined. We sat and chatted for about an hour. His honesty warmed me to him.

I thought I could help this man. He was a mirror image of myself some 25 years ago. So I agreed to take him on. Little did I know then that John would become the most difficult client I have ever had, and yet would prove to be the most beneficial to me in terms of my own emotional and spiritual growth. As I have already stated, my method of helping is to set up a two-way dialogue. So we agreed upon a day and time for our first session.

John arrived at our first session with what could best be described as the weight of the world upon his shoulders. Almost immediately he proceeded to inform me of his past sessions of therapy, both in and outside locked units. In brief he had several prison sentences and admissions to both secure and unsecure establishments. He had used domestic violence in all his relationships as his preferred method of getting what he wanted from others. All in all, John was most certainly a reflection of me in earlier times, and presented me with a massive personal challenge. As I observed John I could detect cracks in his emotional make up. That was encouraging.

We agreed that he would write his life story and meet in two weeks time. John decided he needed that time to recall all the past events that made up his life experience to date.

Life story session: John arrived looking very angry and tearful, and he tried to smile but he looked thoroughly rejected – all in all a pathetic sight. He started to read aloud his life story and he did so falteringly. It was blatantly obvious to me that he had taken his time to write this and it was one of the best presentations of a life story it has been my good fortune to listen to. This was one of the most humbling experiences of my life.

I never fail to see a loving God at work when a human being tells another who they really are. It is a deep display of true courage, faith and trust, and for me a deeply felt feeling of love and gratitude for the orator. Never mind all the Hollywood hype and He-man culture; this for me is true courage: a true He-man.

As you can probably guess there were a lot of issues that came to the fore with John. An expression of 'how did this happen to me?' was apparent on his face, mixed with 'how could I do this to another human being?'

For the first time in John's life he was face-to-face with who he really is, as opposed to who he thought he was. This can be a very frightening state of affairs and it was affecting John deeply. He looked like a little boy lost, and in reality that was who he was. Love had been absent all through his childhood, and had been replaced by violence. His own parents constantly put him down. He was told that he was stupid and would never amount to anything.

He was caught playing with his penis in the bath when he was seven years of age and told by his mother that he was a very dirty and wicked boy and would go to hell. John had uncovered about 32 incidents in his past that were directly responsible for producing the results in life he was experiencing today.

It might be very useful to point out at this juncture that incidents in childhood are affecting your life right now.

Many friends of mine have turned to religion or Christianity as part of their spiritual journey. I see them jumping with joy and halleluiahs for six months or so and then they lose their faith or start procrastinating. Jesus says, 'You can't put a new patch on old cloth' and this I am sorry to say is what some churches do. We all need to clear out all the baggage of our past in order to let in the new. We may need to heal from the past, and you can't do that if you do not know what is wrong with you – this seems perfectly clear to me. I remember once suffering from a bad back and the vicar told me to ask God to heal me.

'You don't need medication,' he said, 'just God!'

I replied, 'Next time you have a toothache, vicar, don't go to the dentist. Ask God to heal you!' I was no longer welcome at that church I am happy to report. Churches have been a sore on my behind all my life, and the hypocrisy that I have witnessed is very frightening. If you want to understand God more fully or get in touch with a God of love, a God with no conditions, I recommend you read *Conversations with God* as soon as you can.

Back to John: the session lasted for about six hours and it felt like ten minutes. We discussed at great length the next step and agreed to meet again in a week's time. John departed looking a lot lighter than when he arrived.

When John and I met on the next session he was bubbling over with excitement and pure joy. It was clear that he was experiencing a power greater than him in his life now. He told me how he came to believe in a power greater than himself. This is what he told me:

'I had an awful tussle with the idea of a God in my life. I mean, how could God even like me, never mind love me? My whole life to date has been one of destruction, lies, a trail of devastation, broken promises, broken bones and broken dreams. But recently I saw something moving on the pavement. I investigated the movement and to my surprise it was a dog. The dog was injured. Must have been hit by a car on the road nearby. I suddenly found myself cradling the dog, something I have never done. The dog died in my arms. To my utter disbelieve I was in tears! Crying over a dog! What is going on here? I don't care about anything or anybody! I buried the dog as best as I could, vowing to come back with a spade and do it properly. As I continued with my walk, I could not get this dog incident out of my mind. Then suddenly I realised that this dog had lay dying on his own for I don't know how long and somehow I met him and he did not die on his own. What is that all about? I asked myself. A feeling came over me that was so warm and comforting, it alarmed me. I know now it was a higher power letting me know that I was loved, just as the dog was and I was in tears again. I had met love for the first time head on. God had overwhelmed me with the power of love and I knew somehow that all would be all right with me from now onwards. Don't ask me how I know – I just do and it is absolutely amazing.'

It was another brilliant session with John. I was dealing with a completely different person now, a resurrected John. It is such a joy to observe the recovery of a client. It was good for me as I was able to connect with an incident in my life that I had completely over looked, and I was able to deal with the matter.

I hope by now that you can see how an honest approach to the Nine Keys can and will transform your life no matter what your present circumstances may be. I feel very strongly that the God of my understanding supervised the writing of this book and provided me with the courage required to admit globally my past mistakes.

I don't know about you but when I look at a star lit night, I feel that I can see God's footprint. In truth today I see God's footprint in everything. I hope that you are finding the cases helpful and encouraging. Now I come to the last, but not least, story of a young woman called Mary – a woman of extraordinary courage.

I first met Mary in the autumn (or fall, as my American friends would say) in the year 1993. She was another referral from a past client, and it's worth saying here that this is how I get all my clients these days.

I first talked to Mary over the phone. She was very chatty and articulate, and we arranged to meet the following week for a chat.

My first meeting with Mary on a face-to-face basis was quite interesting and we agreed that we would work together through the Nine Keys.

I think the most striking feature of Mary would have to be her smile: it could light up any dark room. Her life story was to me very illuminating and I knew almost instantly that we could work together. So here is a little bit about Mary and her journey through the Nine Keys.

Mary worked in a home as a care assistant with the elderly. She had worked there for five years, and was not happy working there; she had taken to having fake illnesses rather than go into work.

Mary was very surprised to discover through her life story that she actually wanted to work with animals. As a child she had wanted to be a vet, and she loved horses. Although she never owned a horse, a friend did and she learnt to ride and muck out with her. She could clean the tackle, brush the horse and also saddle the animal and she really enjoyed that.

I asked her why she never studied to be a vet and follow her dream. This is what she told me.

'My mother and father got divorced when I was nine and my whole life just seemed to stop, I was confused and frightened and I wondered if it was my fault that they got divorced. I started to mix with the wrong crowd, one thing led to another and I found myself in trouble with the police for unruly behaviour. I started playing truant and going to the park on my own, just to watch other families and to cry. All the relationships that I tried to have ended in my boyfriends just walking away from me.'

Mary's self-worth was zero.

It was a very long and powerful session. We worked for about six hours. Mary was able to isolate her problems and to re-evaluate their significance on her life today.

It is always surprising to me the positive effect on a person's life once they have brought their secrets out into the open and shared them with another. They may have been festering deep within for many years, controlling the life of the individual and as often as not limiting their quality of life.

This is why writing your life story is so important in my opinion, as it can uncover hidden barriers in all areas of your life. Misunderstood parental transactions often result in guilt or fear – and this becomes your automatic reaction to situations in your adult life, and cause you pain today. We had four sessions on Mary's life story. When it felt right to move to the next Key we did.

Mary already had faith in a God of the church, but not one of her own – one of love. She never had a personal relationship with a higher power; she never believed that she could have one.

However, after reading some of the suggested readings she developed a very personal relationship with her God.

Mary was able to forgive herself and all the others who had impacted her life up to this day. She said, and I quote:

'I felt a great weight being lifted from me.
I could float in love and it is a miracle.'

Mary made a list of things that she wanted to change in her life, the first being her job. She also wanted to change some of her companions, the negative ones. The most important thing that she wanted to change, however, was her mindset; her perception of life.

It is a gift from the universe to be able to help someone help himself, or herself, and begin to transform his or her life. For me personally it is a very humbling experience and helps me keep my feet on the ground.

You can transform your life. The cases I have briefly outlined did just that and so can you. Are you willing to try? Hey! What have you got to lose?

It is my intention to go on the road to meet as many people as I can to introduce the Nine Keys and also the new spirituality. I feel that it is a matter of some urgency.

There are many people suffering today who will benefit from taking the journey.

I have developed a one-day workshop specifically designed to introduce this programme and I also intend to hold four day spiritual retreats/workshops – so who knows, we may meet personally one day. That would be just fabulous. If we never meet, you are still in my heart. You are a wonderfully unique child of the universe and you are loved.

SUGGESTED READINGS

Conversations with God, Neale Donald Walsch

The Last Hours of Ancient Sunlight, Thom Hartmann

Conscious Evolution, Barbara Marx Hubbard

Reworking Success, Robert Theobald

The Celestine, Vision James Redfield

The Politics of Meaning, Michael Lemer

The Future of Love, Daphne Rose Kingma

Diet for a New America, John Robbins

The Four Agreements, Don Miguel Ruiz

The Power of Now, Eckhart Tolle

When Bad Things Happen to Good People, Rabbi Harold Kushner

Anatomy of an Illness, Norman Cousins

The Power of Positive Thinking, Dr. Norman Vincent Peale

Transforming Pain Into Power, Dr. Doris Helge

Autobiography of a Yogi, Paramahansa Yogananda

The Nature of Personal Reality, Jane Roberts

Anatomy of the Spirit, Carolyn Myss

Practical Spirituality, John Randolph Price

lllusions, Richard Bach

Love is Letting Go of Fear, Gerald Jampolsky

Handbook to Higher Consciousness, Ken Keyes Jr.

Return to Love, Marianne Williamson

A Course in Miracles, Foundation for Inner Peace

The Celestine Prophecy, James Redfield

What You Think of Me is None of My Business, Terry Cole-Whitaker

Stephen Lives, Anne Puryear

The Universe is a Green Dragon, Brian Swimme

The Unimaginable Lie, Kenny and Julia Loggins

As a Man Thinketh, James Allen

Life After Life, Dr. Raymond Moody

The Way of the Peaceful Warrior, Dan Millman

The Holographic Universe, Michael Talbot

Paths to Love, Deepak Chopra

Many Lives, Many Masters, Dr. Brian Weiss

All is You, Kermit Kuczola

Seat of the Soul, Gary Zukav

You Can Heal Your Life, Louise Hay

Creative Visualization, Shakti Gawain

Stranger in a Strange Land, Robert Heinlein

There surely is enough reading here to occupy your mind and to keep you happy for a while at least, eh?

CONTACT THE AUTHOR

Finally, I would just like to express my joy in talking to you – it has been an absolute privilege for me. My remit for all of this is simply this: if I have helped one person to transform their life, then all of this has been worthwhile. May your journey be a source of enlightenment, may you feel rewarded in your endeavours and until we chat again may the God of your understanding go with you.

I am currently working on my next book. The working title is: *The Last Tears.* This book deals with my all the events in my life that led to me becoming homeless and on the streets. On reflection there were many warning signs that I never noticed or chose to ignore. It deals with the violence, addiction, failures, losses and so forth. My final book has the working title *Coffee with God and Tea with the Devil?* This books deals with our duality and perhaps will help us to understand more fully why we do the things we do, when we never intended to do them. It will deal with the opposites: love-hate, joy-sadness, abundance-poverty etc.

So I am looking forward to talking to you again.

Feel free to contact me by email: sandy41@blueyonder.co.uk, or visit my website: www.sandydonaghy.com

May your God go with you in your daily life.

Love, Blessings – Sandy